Dante

A Brief History

D1394497

BLACKWELL BRIEF HISTORIES OF RELIGION SERIES

This series offers brief, accessible, and lively accounts of key topics within theology and religion. Each volume presents both academic and general readers with a selected history of topics which have had a profound effect on religious and cultural life. The word "history" is, therefore, understood in its broadest cultural and social sense. The volumes are based on serious scholarship but they are written engagingly and in terms readily understood by general readers.

Published

Alister E. McGrath – *Heaven*
G. R. Evans – *Heresy*
Tamara Sonn – *Islam*
Douglas J. Davies – *Death*
Lawrence S. Cunningham – *Saints*
Carter Lindberg – *Christianity*
Peter S. Hawkins – *Dante*

Dante

A Brief History

Peter S. Hawkins

BLACKWELL PUBLISHING
350 Main Street, Malden, MA 02148-5020, USA
9600 Garsington Road, Oxford OX4 2DQ UK
550 Swanston Street, Carlton, Victoria 3053, Australia

First published 2006 by Blackwell Publishing Ltd

2   2010

Library of Congress Cataloging-in-Publication Data

Hawkins, Peter S.
  A brief history of Dante / Peter S. Hawkins.
    p. cm.—(Blackwell brief histories of religion)
  Includes bibliographical references and index.
  ISBN 978-1-4051-3051-6 (hardcover : alk paper)
  ISBN 978-1-4051-3052-3 (pbk. : alk. paper)

  1. Dante Alighieri, 1265–1321. 2. Authors, Italian—To 1500—Biography.
I. Title. II. Series.
PQ4335.H39 2006
851'.1—dc22
[B]
                                                    2005030635

A catalogue record for this title is available from the British Library.

Set in 10pt/12pt Meridian
by SPI publisher services, Pondicherry, India

Picture Research by Kitty Bocking

For further information on
Blackwell Publishing, visit our website:
www.blackwellpublishing.com

For Phyllis Carol Depp Cook, who for 30 years of friendship has awaited this book.

Praise for *Dante: A Brief History*

''Peter Hawkins unveils Dante the writer and the person. He does so not only with impeccable scholarship but also with emotion, common sense, and empathy – all expressed in beautifully clear prose. Moreover, Hawkins reminds us that Dante does not belong exclusively to scholars and specialists: here, new 'pilgrims' are welcomed aboard. Those who revisit the *Commedia* under his guidance will be reminded anew why the poet remains prominently on our shelves, and will place this volume right alongside it.''

Matthew Pearl, author of The Dante Club

''Peter Hawkins' knowledge of and passion for Dante shines through every page of this elegantly written book. He writes, moreover, with passion and precision. This is not only a superb introduction to Dante, but a work which will move and enlighten those thoroughly steeped in a poet who remains, seven centuries after his death, still very much our contemporary.''

Gabriel Josipivici, University of Sussex

''A wonderful book for the awe and wonder that the author brings to his personal reading of the poem and which he also inspires in the reader. His perceptions convey the 'aliveness' not only of Dante's poem but equally of his own critical imagination.''

Richard Lansing, Brandeis University

''Anyone who makes Dante and his genius more available to modern readers deserves our thanks. Peter Hawkins' careful reading and meticulous scholarship not only brings Dante to life but also shows how he has touched and enlivened readers throughout the ages. Dante's vision never ceases to challenge and deepen us and the *Commedia* speaks to our age as much as it did to his. The great thing about this book is that it makes one want to go out and read or re-read the original story. Readers tend to project their own prejudices and longings onto the poet. But Dante is always ahead of us, as if to say with Beatrice, 'Look and look well,' you will never get to the bottom of things. A timely message in a dangerous age of raucous certainties.''

Alan Jones, Dean of Grace Cathedral, San Francisco
and author of The Soul's
Journey: The Three Passages of the Spiritual Life
with Dante as Guide.

Contents

Illustrations

Acknowledgments

I was thrilled when Rebecca Harkin of Blackwell Publishers invited me to be part of a series aimed at bringing complicated subjects to the "general educated reader" – people with interest but without expertise. Would I do such a book on Dante? For 30 years I have been writing on the poet for Dantisti, my professional peers. Here was a chance to do in print what I have tried to do in the classroom, first at Yale Divinity School and now at Boston University. My task would be not so much to learn new things about Dante – although, in fact, writing this book has taught me a great deal about the poet I did not know before – but rather finding a way to avoid the "in-house" aspect of so much Dante criticism, no doubt including my own. If I have succeeded, it has been with the help of "general educated reader" friends who helped me see what made no sense to them, what they wanted to know more about, and how I might want to say this or that if I truly had them in mind. A number gave me feedback on a given chapter, for which I am grateful; but those who worked their way through the whole manuscript deserve thanks by name: Cristine Hutchison-Jones, Michael Hendrickson, and Stephen Henderson (who, with a journalist's fierce economy, warned me against the perils of baggy academic prose). My closest

Dante colleague, Rachel Jacoff, kept me responsible on the home front.

"Home," however, was not where I wrote this book. Throughout the sabbatical year 2004–05 afforded me by Boston University, I was a perpetual guest. Dante too was on the road when he wrote the *Commedia* but suffered acutely from a sense of dislocation. On the contrary, my temporary "exile" from Boston provided me with one of the happiest years of my life, thanks to the kindness of those who supported and housed me. Bruce Redford and Dennis Crawley loaned me their Provincetown condo. Michael Malone and Maureen Quilligan turned over their Connecticut house with its beatific view of a tidal river. I spent a blissful month at the Bogliasco Foundation's Ligurian Study Center just south of Genoa and overlooking the aptly named Golfo Paradiso. Then there were five months as Starr Fellow at Oxford's Lady Margaret Hall, where Principal Frances Lannon and the rest of the college made me feel as if I were truly on home territory. Finally, Andrea Nightingale turned over her California house and garden, as she has generously done in the past, only this time with the happy addition of a tiger cat named Jamalia Sweets.

My great hope for this *Brief History of Dante* is that it will give my readers as much pleasure as I found in writing it.

Abbreviations

All biblical references are to the Douay Reims English translation of the Vulgate; all citations of the *Commedia* are from the bilingual edition of Allen Mandelbaum, 3 vols. New York: Bantam Books, 1982. References to other works by Dante are based on the following editions, which are indicated throughout by the abbreviations given here:

Alighieri, Dante.

Conv.	*The Banquet (Convivio).*Trans. Christopher Ryan. Stanford French and Italian Studies 61. Saratoga, CA: ANMA Libri, 1989.
Epist.	*Dantis Alagherii Epistolae: The Letters of Dante*. Ed. Paget Toynbee, 2nd edn. Oxford: Clarendon Press, 1966.
VN	*Vita Nuova. Italian Text with Facing English Translation*. Eds. Dino Cervigni and Edward Vasta. Notre Dame, IN: University of Notre Dame Press, 1995.

The following abbreviations are also used:

Inf.	*Inferno*
Purg.	*Purgatorio*
Par.	*Paradiso*

CCD	*The Cambridge Companion to Dante*. Ed. Rachel Jacoff. Cambridge, UK: Cambridge University, 1993.
D & MA	*Dante and the Middle Ages*. Eds. John C. Barnes and Cormac Ó Cuilleanáin, Published for The Foundation for Italian Studies University College, Dublin. Dublin: Irish Academic Press, 1995.
DCH	*Dante, The Critical Heritage (1314(?) –1870)*. Ed. Michael Caesar, The Critical Heritage Series. London and New York: Routledge, 1989.
DCP	*Dante: Contemporary Perspectives*. Ed. Amilcare A. Iannucci. Toronto: University of Toronto Press, 1997.
DCT	*Dante, Cinema and Television*. Ed. Amilcare A. Iannucci. Toronto: University of Toronto Press, 2004.
DE	*Dante Encyclopedia*. Ed. Richard Lansing. New York: Garland, 2000.
DEL	*Dante in English Literature*. Ed. Paget Toynbee. 2 vols. London: Methuen, 1909.
DM	*Dante Metamorphoses. Episodes in a Literary Afterlife*. Ed. Eric Haywood. Dublin: Four Courts Press, 2003.
DMA	*Dante's Modern Afterlife: Reception and Response from Blake to Heaney*. Ed. Nick Havely. New York: St. Martin's Press, 1998.
DNM	*Dante for the New Millenium*. Eds. Teodolinda Barolini and H. Wayne Storey. New York: Fordham University Press, 2003.
PD	*The Poets' Dante: Twentieth-Century Responses*. Eds. Peter S. Hawkins and Rachel Jacoff. New York: Farrar, Straus and Giroux, 2001.

Prologue: Invitation to a Reader

"Why is Dante so difficult?" These are reputedly the last words spoken by the seventeenth-century Spanish playwright, Calderón de la Barca. Even in the often bizarre annals of deathbed sayings, this utterance is surprising on several counts. In the first place, Calderón was renowned for the extreme obscurity of his own work, which doubles the implicit indictment made against Dante. But second, given all that might flood a mind on the brink of death, why was Calderón having even a passing thought about the author of the *Commedia*? One might expect that so fiercely pious a Catholic would rely on the assurances of the Church at this threshold moment.

Maybe he sensed, however, that Dante knew something more about the "undiscovered country" than did the priest at his bedside. And if the wisdom of poets is to be trusted at all, who else to turn to than the undisputed master of the Christian afterlife? It was Dante, after all, who bequeathed to western culture the most vivid, detailed sense of what may await us beyond the grave.

Yet frankly, who wants to be confronted with "difficulty" when in extremis, or even in the best of times? To be sure, some like a challenge, say a certain kind of precocious high school student whose literature teacher throws down the gauntlet early on. "We turn now to T. S. Eliot," said Mr Varriale, my 11th-grade English teacher, "the most difficult poet in the English language." At the time, none of us could make any sense out of *The Waste Land,* even with the notes Eliot provided or with those that generations of scholars have added. The most ambitious of us looked up the references, hunted for symbols, started fooling with Tarot cards, repeated "Shantih shantih shantih" – *anything* that might give a clue to Eliot's meaning. Cynical classmates smirked at our efforts and assured us that the whole thing was a hoax. The "most difficult poet in the English language" had no clothes.

The problem with Dante is something different: he has too many clothes, too much meaning. Homer and the Bible, for instance, are far older and come from worlds substantially more remote than Dante's early fourteenth-century Florence. While a reading of the *Odyssey* or the Gospel of Mark can certainly be enhanced by introductions and footnotes, in neither case is such assistance necessary. The oldest story we possess, the five-thousand-year-old *Epic of Gilgamesh,* is replete with unfamiliar names but otherwise seems timeless. These texts pretty much speak for themselves.

So too, one might think, should the *Commedia*. It has a story line that could hardly be more straightforward: Dante is lost, found, and then led along a journey that takes him through the three realms of the afterlife until, in the final moment, he is enraptured into God's presence. Furthermore, we know how the story ends right away: the complete itinerary is given in the opening canto. It may take 14,233 lines to tell but its message is a familiar one. The hymn "Amazing Grace" sums it up in a few words: "I once was lost but now am found, was blind but now I see."

Though the poem's *vera via* or "true way" is clear, it is still very easy to lose one's bearings and become befuddled in the poem's dense thicket. With more than 14,000 trees, one can lose sight of the "forest" entirely. And a pathless thicket it can seem! A roll call of unfamiliar names, a succession of personal encounters, constant allusions to literature not read, and long-forgotten people and events. The sheer topicality is also infuriating. Dante assumes that "la futura gente," future people who turn his pages, will be able to keep track of (and care about) the medieval nonentities who never had fame's 15 minutes apart from the attention the poet paid them. The shelf life of Florentine politics seems especially short, and one requires remarkable patience to keep track of Guelphs and Ghibellines, Bianchi and Neri, or the catastrophic jilting of the Amidei bride by the Buondelmonte groom in the spring of 1215. Too much information!

For this reason, unlike the spare notes one finds in a contemporary Homer or in any publication of the American Bible Society (with its dedication to presenting the text "without commentary"), new editions of the *Commedia* offer pages of footnotes and compendia, charts and bibliographies, that often exceed the poetic text. Nor is the annotated poem something new, a necessary concession to the deficiencies of our culture. The poet's corpse was barely cold before commentary began, and his sons, Jacopo and Pietro, were the first to have a hand at a scholarly industry that has continued unabated ever since.

As someone who has worked hard to join himself to this enterprise I like to think that the impulse to comment is more generous than controlling, a genuine attempt to share Dante's wealth by unearthing otherwise buried treasure. Moreover, in a poem in which the solitary protagonist is rescued in the first half of the opening canto, and then never left without a guide for the 99 cantos to follow, it makes a kind of poetic justice for the commentator to hold the reader's hand at every turn, filling in gaps in knowledge, connecting the dots. Unfortunately, such "helpfulness" can make the reader feel that the *Commedia* is too arduous by half. Why bother?

Because, as I hope the following pages will substantiate, Dante is well worth the effort. Always difficult, he has always succeeded in winning over his readers. We see this in the explosion of manuscripts in the poet's own fourteenth century, as well as an ongoing (if uneven) readership over the last seven hundred years. Thanks in part to Dante's literary achievement (and those of Giovanni Boccaccio and Francesco Petrarch soon after him), the poem's *volgare illustre fiorentino*, its "illustrious Florentine vernacular," was accepted by the sixteenth century simply as "Italian." Russian poet Osip Mandelstam put it this way: "Dante's creation [was] above all the entrance of the language of his day onto the world stage, its entrance as a totality, as a system" (*PD*, p. 43).

In our own era, he seems to have come into his own in English, a language he probably never heard (despite a legend that he traveled to Oxford), as well as in dialects spoken on continents unimaginable on his world map. More than 20 English translations have appeared since World War II on both sides of the Atlantic, together with a plethora of critical writing, more than a few *Commedia*-inflected movies and plays, plus Matthew Pearl's recent best-selling novel that re-creates the world of the Longfellow "Dante Club" in mid-nineteenth-century Boston.

Italians come to the *Commedia* as compulsory reading in high school. A year is devoted to each realm of the afterlife, and the whole business is often undertaken by students (and perhaps by their teachers) with the enthusiasm of those sentenced to hard labor. Moreover, Dante in Italy is a pop icon as well as a cultural high-water mark: not only does he give his name to brands of butter and olive oil, but the Internet search engine equivalent of "Google" is "virgilio.it." Outside Italy, and apart from a pop cultural presence in the United States (see Chapter 5), exposure to the *Commedia* is hit or miss. My own first direct encounter was as a freshman in college, when I worked my way through a paperback *Inferno* along with other masterpieces of "Western World Literature" before consigning them all to oblivion. The poem left no impression.

I tried again two years later, during summer school, when a study of the entire *Commedia* in translation seemed to be an ideal choice for beach reading. It was not. My lively Italian instructor had a native speaker's love for the language, which alas none of us could share. The poem appeared as a kind of Rosetta Stone: a text to be deciphered and a cultural monument to be revered. But I have never been much interested in puzzles, and monuments invariably invite my skepticism. They usually are smaller and less compelling than reported.

Some texts may require readers "of a certain age." If truth be told, at 20 I was too immature to enter into Dante's world. A scrawl I then left in the margin of my *Purgatorio* is telling. At the end of canto 27, Dante and Virgil, after journeying down through Hell and then up the winding path of the purgatorial mountain, stand on the brink of Eden. On the edge of Paradise regained, Virgil bids his "son," the pilgrim, goodbye – words that turn out to be his last in the *Commedia*. In this valediction Virgil offers both a summation of what Dante's learned over the long course of their journey together and of the person he's become:

> My son, you've seen the temporary fire
> and the eternal fire; you have reached
> the place past which my powers cannot see.
>
> I've brought you here through intellect and art;
> from now on, let your pleasure be your guide;
> you're past the steep and past the narrow paths.

> Look at the sun that shines upon your brow;
> look at the grasses, flowers, and the shrubs
> born here, spontaneously, of the earth.
>
> Among them, you can rest or walk until
> the coming of the glad and lovely eyes –
> those eyes that, weeping, sent me to your side.
>
> Await no further word or sign from me:
> your will is free, erect, and whole – to act
> against that will would be to err: therefore
>
> I crown and miter you over yourself.
>
> (*Purg.* 27. 127–42)

Even after many years of teaching the *Commedia*, I still savor this moment with my students and see my own vocation afresh. It no doubt has resonance with anyone who has given his or her best to someone younger, and then recognized (a tear in the eye) that it is now time to let go. How could it be, then, that in the margin of that now-yellowed *Purgatorio* there appears a single word written in pencil in what I recognize to be my youthful handwriting: "Yawn."

What was I thinking? Was this some adolescent peevishness on my part, a "Yawn" of defiance against a teacher going on about poignancy? Or was it a measure of my youthful incapacity to feel what it was like to part with my beloved teachers, to lose parents and lovers and friends, or to experience the bittersweet rapture of moving on? Obviously, I could not imagine that in decades to come a student might even have me in mind when she or he reflected on Virgil's words.

I was fortunate several years later to be given another (by this time, third) chance. I had intended to visit a Yale graduate seminar on Dante but then only at the behest of a friend and only for the first session. Instead, I audited the class for the entire year, filling the margins of my bilingual edition with notes, and resolving that come the summer I would learn how to read the Italian. A year later my doctoral thesis on Edmund

Spenser's *Faerie Queene* was held hostage to Dante, much to the consternation of the English department faculty who did not recognize the poet as one of their own. Against the odds – I was not a trained medievalist or all that proficient in Italian – I resolved to devote myself to a poem that seemed not only to include the world but to be a world in itself. Nothing else I had encountered in literature was as pressed down and overflowing as this text.

What accounts for this turning from indifference to passion? An excellent teacher, no doubt, and brilliant classmates who later became colleagues and fellow travelers through the *Commedia*. Then there was Dante's vivid, unconventional presentation of the Christian tradition when I was looking for a more compelling experience of faith than I'd known. Most of all, at a time when I was deeply in love and trying to understand the larger ramifications of my Eros, I'd found a story of a human love rooted in God.

Over the last 30-odd years, of course, my relationship both to poem and poet has evolved. I have taken on, at least to some degree, the "hermeneutics of suspicion." A less enthralled and therefore more querulous reader, I'm now disinclined always to take the poet at his word or let his authorial sleights of hand go unnoticed. The *Commedia*, for all its stupefying inner coherence, seems less airtight; it appears to me not so much a miracle as a stunning achievement. Yet this critical distance has in no way diminished my love for the text. What is less airtight allows room to breathe; the more human the poet becomes, the more astonishing appears the divinity he is able to suggest within and between his gorgeous lines.

I have permitted myself this extended autobiographical aside to encourage prospective readers who have been put off by the poet's much vaunted difficulty. I wish as well to invite back those who once picked up the book and then – mired in the *Inferno*'s horror or flummoxed by the *Paradiso*'s theology – decided to put it back on the shelf. "Take it and read, take it and read," sang the childish voice Augustine heard in the Milanese garden of *Confessions* 8, when he heeded this cry and found himself changed forever. Readers of Dante have nothing to lose in coming to the *Commedia* – except, perhaps, life as they've known it thus far.

After beginning with my own history, it makes a certain sense to turn immediately in Chapter 1 to a brief account of Dante's life (1265–1321). After all, it is the compelling nature of his personal story – the urgency of his address, his intimacy with his readers, how his confession elicits one's own – that draws us in and keeps us reading. My hope is that this over-view will give the newcomer a sense of competence when confronting the footnotes and apparatus of a standard edition of the poem.[1] And, because everything I have to say in this *Brief History* will depend on some overall sense of what Dante is up to in all three canticles of the *Commedia* (*Inferno*, *Purgatorio*, and *Paradiso*), Chapter 2 will retell *its* story. Those who have not yet picked up the poem will find at least a sketch of the big picture; for those who already have it at least some-where in mind, this exposition of the poem's territory may be a useful supplement. No doubt another Dantista would give a quite different account, with other observations and em-phases. For better or worse, this is my story, my version of the song.

Because my own particular interest is in Dante's religious sensibility rather than his political thought or literary inven-tion, the next two chapters focus on the theological dimension of his work. Chapter 3 looks at the figure of Beatrice as she takes shape throughout Dante's writing, and at the range of issues the poet addresses through her. The one that particu-larly intrigues me was the most innovative in his time and is the most neglected in our own: the function of Eros in the spiritual life. Chapter 4 probes Dante's take on Christian theology, paying particular attention to those aspects and expressions of faith that are characteristic, maybe even idiosyncratic, to him.

Finally, Chapter 5 will suggest how over the centuries Dante has been variously ''constructed'' – as lover, statesman, neo-Platonist, proto-Protestant, Romantic visionary, Byronic hero, Pre-Raphaelite, father of his country, theologian in verse, precursor of the modern novel, and, finally, *altissimo poeta*, the consummate poet. Here I'll explore the *Commedia*'s afterlife, its reception over the centuries (especially in the English-speaking world), and its impact on contemporary culture. On the basis of what previous generations have found in Dante, readers may have a sense of what may be in store for them – the gift or the challenge they'll take away from the text.

So what do we make of Calderón de la Barca's alleged final words, ''Why is Dante so difficult?'' If I dare to conjure up my own ''play's last scene,'' phrases remembered from poems, like the one just cited from Donne's *Holy Sonnets*, may well inform my death as they do my living. Then again, I rather doubt that in such a moment I will be worrying much about literature. Surely there will be memories of my family, of things done and left undone, recollections from the spectrum of pleasure and pain, from love-making to kidney stones. I hope someone will anoint me, and someone else rub my feet. As I turn toward the life to come, part of me anticipates angels and archangels, white-robed elders and clouds of incense, ten thousand times ten thousand crying out, ''Holy, Holy, Holy.'' Another me, child of a skeptical age, imagines only a blank screen.

But what about the author on whom I've spent a good deal of my life? If I speak of him, what might I say? Bystanders strain to hear what may well be my last words. It is not easy to pick them up. However, the nurse who is on duty, with her well-trained ear, is certain she understands what I've muttered. The words themselves do not make very much sense to her, but together they form a question: "I wonder … if Dante got it … right … after all?"

Chapter 1

Dante's Life and Works

Any study of Dante must begin with the man himself: there is no getting around him. Indeed, Dante has made it impossible for us *not* to look for him or read his work as autobiographical. In almost all of his writing, major and minor, there is the inescapable sense of a singular individual quite willing to self-dramatize. He talks about himself freely despite a professed hesitation about doing so (*Conv.* 1.2), or even about registering his own name (*Purg.* 30.62–3). Yet this demurral is pure smoke screen: no writer ever made such good use of the ''I'' as Dante. We have every right to hunt for hints of what he felt and thought, at least insofar as we can ever separate out the voices of poet and pilgrim from the ''real'' Dante Alighieri who crafted them both.

Domenico da Michelino understood this very well (see Figure 1). In 1465, the second centenary of Dante's birth, he was commissioned to produce a painting for the cathedral in Florence; it still hangs there, on the north wall of the Duomo's nave.[1] Michelino gives us the towering figure of the poet looking like a saint in a conventional religious painting. Instead of holding an open Bible, however, he tenders the *Commedia*, its first page radiant with light. Both poet and text are turned to face his birthplace, which is crowded with the splendid monuments unknown in Dante's day but familiar to Michelino and his fellow-citizens two hundred years later. While the painter shows him looking leftward toward Florence, he points with his right hand to the open gates of Hell – a warning to those inside the city of the fate to befall any who ignore the "scripture" he holds out to them. This gigantic image of Dante is placed in a stylized wilderness that no doubt represents the exile to which Florence subjected him. In the rear of the painting we see the Mountain of Purgatory, and above it a suggestion of the heavenly spheres through which the pilgrim ascends in

Figure 1   Domenico da Michelino, ''Dante and his poem''
Alinari Archives, Florence

the *Paradiso*. There is no missing the fact, at least to the mind of one fifteenth-century artist, that the poet and his writing make a single picture.

The relevance of the man to the work is most obviously seen in the *Commedia*, in which Dante is both the narrator of the story (''the poet'') and the protagonist within the narrative (''the pilgrim''). This is also the case in his first book, the *Vita Nuova*, in which Dante-as-poet looks into his ''book of memory'' and, in both prose and poetry, meditates on the impact of a woman called Beatrice upon his youthful life. While the autobiographical thrust of Dante's other works is not so striking, it in fact characterizes *De Vulgari Eloquentia*, *Convivio*, and *Monarchia*, each of which will be touched on presently. His epistles, needless to say, are in some sense all about him. To different extents, then, everything Dante wrote presupposes the sheer drama of his life.

The Life Story

The poet's biography has been written many times over, starting a mere 20 years or so after his death. First there was the brief account by the great chronicler of Florence, Giovanni Villani (c.1348). Then, in about 1360, Giovanni Boccaccio circulated his treatise in praise of the poet, the *Trattatello in laude di Dante*.[2] To begin, Villani paints the portrait of a great citizen and polymath but also something of an antisocial snob: ''This Dante, because of his knowledge, was somewhat haughty and reserved and disdainful, and after the fashion of a philosopher, careless of graces and not easy in his converse with laymen'' (*DCH*, pp. 150–1). Boccaccio takes these unappealing attributes into account but accentuates the positive. He celebrates Dante the genius; he also gives us what becomes the received notion of what the poet looked like: ''His face was long, his nose aquiline, and his eyes rather large than small; his jaws big, and the underlip protruding beyond the upper. His complexion was dark, his hair and beard thick, black, and curling, and his expression very melancholy and thoughtful" (*DCH*, p. 163). This is the image, famously painted by Raphael, that remained fixed in people's minds until a painting thought to be by Giotto, presumably taken from life, was discovered in Florence in 1840 (see Figure 2). Suddenly, the brooding hook-nosed Dante, "the mask of a corpse of 56," became a "fine noble young man" who might well have fought a battle on horseback or wooed a lady with sonnets (*DEL*, 2, p. 640).

Not much can be said securely about Dante's origins or early life. The Alighieri family was "old," at least to the poet's mind. In *Paradiso* 15, Cacciaguida, his great-great-grandfather, traces the line back to the Roman Elisei clan, allegedly one of the founding families of Florence. Dante celebrates his

Figure 2 Detail of Dante Alighieri in *Paradiso*
Finsiel/Alinari Archives, Florence

ancestry throughout these cantos in the Heaven of Mars. Yet we also hear Cacciaguida noting that Dante's great-grand-father Alighiero *continues* to circle the Terrace of Pride centuries after his death (*Par*. 15.91–6) – a subtle indication that Dante came by his own enormous ego quite naturally. Nor are we allowed to miss Beatrice's indulgent smile at the pilgrim as he revels in his ''roots,'' or the voice of the poet, coming from off stage, remarking on how little ''nobility of blood'' turns out to matter (*Par*. 16.1–15). As usual, Dante has it both ways: he manages to be proud *and* humble at the same time.

About Alighiero Alighieri, Dante's father, the poet is completely silent. Neither the man nor his house seem to have been very important, though the properties he held both in the city and surrounding countryside were sufficient to underwrite Dante's Florentine life and creative work. In addition to being a notary, Alighiero seems to have functioned as a money-changer and lender, like Dante's uncle Brunetto and grandfather Bellicione. In a boom town like thirteenth-century Florence, steadily outgrowing its ancient walls and conducting trade with much of the known world, such a profession could be very lucrative. It was also vaguely shameful in an ostensibly Christian culture that professed to abhor usury.

The shadow of illicit paternal wealth would fall on Dante both before and after his exile. But it is also true that his father's massed resources enabled him after his 30th year to join a guild (physicians and apothecaries), to become active in the political life of the commune, and to devote his creative energies to poetry. There seems also to have been some military service in the 1289 Florentine campaign against the city of Arezzo, whose cavalry assault the poet recalls vividly in *Inferno* 22.4–9 (''I have seen / rangers and raiding parties galloping''), if in the hilarious context of mock epic.[3]

Of the poet's maternal lineage there is even less to say. Again according to Cacciaguida (*Par*. 15.136–8), the Alighieri family name derived from Dante's mother's side. Bella died when her son was only six, and it's tempting to imagine the extraordinary warmth he accords to the mother–child relationship, especially in the latter part of the *Paradiso*, as compensation for this loss.

The other female important to Dante's early life was Gemma Donati, offspring of a far nobler family, to whom he was betrothed in 1277, when he was only 12. They were later married and together had four children, three boys (Giovanni, Pietro, and Jacopo) and a girl (Antonia, who assumed the name Beatrice when she became a nun). Boccaccio described the marriage as a disaster – a judgment that a fifteenth-century biographer, Leonardo Bruni, dismissed entirely. Who knows? In his writings Dante says nothing about either his wife or children. Adult sons were often forced to join their fathers in exile. Jacopo and Pietro, together with Antonia, seemed to have made that decision for themselves by going to Ravenna at what turned out to be the end of Dante's life. Gemma Donati, however, stayed in Florence. Two of the three sons went on to become interpreters of their father's writing: Jacopo wrote a commentary on the *Inferno* in Italian and Pietro a commentary in Latin on the entire *Commedia*. Pietro later moved to Verona, where his father had spent many years of his exile. He married, became a judge, and on at least one occasion performed a vernacular verse summary of the poem in what became the city's Piazza di Dante.

The Figure of Beatrice

Whatever Dante's marriage to Gemma Donati may have been, and whatever the strength of his ties to his children, the Florentine who made all the difference to his life was Beatrice. We have Boccaccio to thank for first identifying Beatrice as

Bice di Folco Portinari, a daughter of the Portinari and a Bardi by marriage, thus linking her to two prominent Florentine families. She died in 1290 at the age of 24. If Dante's beloved is indeed this same woman, then these bare facts are nearly all that can be reliably said about her. About the Beatrice Dante created, on the other hand, there is a good deal more to say, though infinitely less than one might like.

We have few clues about who she was apart from the lover who immortalized her. According to the *Vita Nuova*, an almost nine-year-old Dante first saw her on May Day 1274 when she was roughly the same age. Nine years later there was another meeting, and life changed irrevocably. Beatrice smiled and he was transfixed; she withheld her salutation, he fell into despair. Much of this is the overheated romanticism of "courtly love," whereby a suitor bewails his inaccessible lady and talks a great deal about himself. When such narcissism is pointed out to the suffering Dante, he takes note and begins to write instead about his lady. He does so in ways that link her not merely to the angelic goddesses whom vernacular poets had hymned before, but, astoundingly, to Christ. This was either romantic hyperbole approaching irreverence or a new way of understanding what a beloved could be for a lover. As the *Vita Nuova* concludes, the young poet vows that someday he will write for Beatrice what no man had yet offered a woman in verse. Fifteen years later the *Commedia* made good on that promise.

The *Vita Nuova* was in circulation by 1295, when Dante turned 30. It consisted of many poems written earlier, independent of one another, but subsequently organized within an autobiographical prose narrative. In their compilation, they seemed freshly wrought to account for the miracle of Beatrice. In this somewhat odd collection of old and new, the author wears many hats: he is poet, memoirist, and literary critic of his own efforts. The intended audience seems to have been his peer group: young men fascinated by philosophy, physiology, and the earlier vernacular poetry of Italy and Provence. First among them, and Dante's declared "primo amico" or best friend, was the poet Guido Cavalcanti: 10 years older, learned, sophisticated, well-born, and inclined to believe that Eros was more an affair of Mars than Venus – more likely to lead to madness and death than anything remotely like divine glory. Dante's *Vita Nuova*, which he refers to as his *libello* or little book, was ostensibly a gift to a mentor and the fruit of a powerful friendship. Yet it was as much written *against* Cavalcanti as for him.

The *Vita Nuova* established Dante – at least according to one of the poet's characters in the *Purgatorio* – as master of the "dolce stil novo" (*Purg*. 24.57), the sweet new style. What distinguished Dante from his literary circle was that he truly took note of what Love breathed within him and then wrote it down. His style might be his own, but (like the inspired authors of Scripture) his words ultimately came from beyond (*Purg*. 24.52–63).

What begins in the *Vita Nuova* as a claim for inspiration – Beatrice sends visions from Heaven that one day will be recorded in verse – then develops over the length of the *Commedia* into something infinitely more audacious. His recollections of the impact of Beatrice upon his youth goes on to become the *Commedia*'s journey to God. The lady not only leads him toward the beatific vision but commands him to write a work that will warn his readers of their headlong rush toward death: "Take note; and even as I speak these words, / do you transmit them to those / who live the life that is a race toward death" (*Purg*. 32.52–4). Dante is a prophet as well as a poet.

Political Life

The year 1295, when the *Vita Nuova* had its debut, also marks Dante's formal entrance into the civic and political world of

Florence. The commune had opened itself to men who were by no means from the elite.[4] Dante's family, like others neither aristocratic nor rich, allied themselves with the republican Guelph party (which looked to the papacy and the French for support of their interests) rather than the imperial Ghibellines (aligned with the Holy Roman Empire). By the time that Dante's membership in a guild gave him formal access to politics, Florence was entirely (and permanently) in the hands of the Guelphs. Yet this fact turned out to mean nothing for civic peace and stability.

In public records Dante appears as a member of various councils that played a part in governing the city. By 1300 – the designated year of the *Commedia*'s journey through the afterlife – he had sufficiently risen in the oligarchy of Florence to be elected to a two-month term as one of the six priors of the commune (one prior for each of the *sesti* or administrative jurisdictions of the city). During their time in office, the priors were sequestered in public quarters. This made sure they would be available for municipal business at all times; it also, no doubt, cut down on lobbying by their constituents. In one sense, this period marks a high point in Dante's life: no other Alighieri had risen to such an office or been given the public trust to this extent. In fact, however, his political success was the beginning of the end.

At this moment, the commune was about to be torn apart by conflict between the dominant Guelph party's two factions, the Bianchi or "Whites" and the Neri, or "Blacks." Historians can find no clear cause for the split between the two in ideology, economic interest, or class (although the "Blacks" regarded themselves as more grand or better established than the allegedly upstart "Whites"). Perhaps what pitted them against one another was what Dante decries throughout in the *Commedia* – a sheer bloody-mindedness, a resolute refusal of partnership no matter the consequences. Although local, this Guelph civil war was connected to larger political strife involving the papacy of Boniface VIII, an increasingly powerful French nation state, and what was left of the Holy Roman Empire. To quell violence that threatened the city during their time in office, the Florentine priors agreed to banish the leaders of the contending factions for a cooling-off period. One of these, Corso Donati, was a relative of Dante's wife Gemma; another was his friend Guido Cavalcanti. This particular order, or at least the way it was carried out, was later said to unjustly favor one side (Cavalcanti's "Whites") over the other (Donati's "Blacks"). Whether or not this perception was true, it had terrible consequences for the poet.

After his priorate, Dante continued to serve the commune in a number of ways. In April 1301 he was put in charge of a road-building project (for which he was later accused of graft); in June he debated against a proposal to assist Pope Boniface in his war against the Aldobrandeschi family. He was asked that September to participate in an embassy to the Vatican on behalf of the Florentine "Whites." Nothing came of the mission. Boniface dismissed the rest of the company after a short time but kept Dante behind for months. As a result, he was powerless to participate in the November 1301 crisis within the commune. The "Blacks" were triumphant, property of the "Whites" was looted or burned, and a punishment was leveled against those who had served the commune in the past. Dante was among them.

By late January of 1302, he and three others were charged with barratry (trafficking in public offices), bribery, taking vengeance against the "Blacks," and other unsubstantiated crimes. He was furthermore denounced for having militated against the papacy on account of its interference in Florentine life – an accusation that was incontrovertibly true! Because Dante did not reply to these charges in person, detained in Rome as he was by Boniface, his property was confiscated, he was exiled for two years, and barred from ever again holding public office. Two months later, another decree condemned him and other former priors to be burned to death should they return to the commune. Others who shared his sentence eventually made their way back to Florence. They accepted the often humiliating terms extended to them and, as best they could, picked up the pieces of their lives. Such was also the case during an earlier period of turmoil for Dante's mentor Brunetto Latini, who went on to become an illustrious figure and office-holder within the city. But for complex reasons, no doubt a mixture of integrity and pride, Dante never went home.

The Work of Exile

Given the extraordinary mobility that characterizes our present-day global society, it may be hard to conceive what exile would have meant to a person as rooted as Dante.[5] Apart from the easily imagined trauma of being separated from family, possessions, and the taken-for-granted securities of daily life and routine, he was losing his identity too. Siena, where he took early refuge along with the many others banished by the new Black Guelph-dominated government, was notoriously an enemy of the Florentines: how could he take up residence *there*? More to the point, Dante did not come from that city or belong to its myth, any more than he did to the other places in north-central Italy he visited during an exile that lasted until his death in 1321 – almost 20 years in duration. In every case the local dialect was different, the food ''off,'' lodging temporary and belonging to someone else. Dante came to know only too well the words that Cacciaguida prophesizes:

> You shall leave everything that you love most dearly:
> this is the arrow that the bow of exile

shoots first. You are to know the bitter taste
  of others' bread, how salt it is, and know
how hard a path it is for one who goes
descending and ascending others' stairs.

                                (Par. 17.55–60)

Cacciaguida goes on to say that among the many crosses to bear in exile, perhaps the heaviest is the company of those who suffered his fate but who had an entirely different heart. They wanted to destroy the city Dante had come to think of as an extension of his own self; they were a crowd that Cacciaguida dismisses as scheming and senseless, insane, completely ungrateful, and profane (*Par.* 17.61–9).

Throughout the *Commedia* the poet accuses Florence of being all these things (and more), so that it may appear that what distinguishes Dante from the "senseless" crowd is the unflappable conviction of his own righteousness. There is rage aplenty in the *Commedia*, but at the work's passionate core burns a frustrated love that refuses resignation and is incapable of the "peace that passes understanding." Nor can we take comfort in Cacciaguida's final word: "your honor will be best kept if your party is yourself" (*Par.* 17.68–9). For a political animal like Dante, with his deeply held belief that to be truly human was to be a "member incorporate" of a community, the prospect of an existence alone – "per te stesso," in Cacciaguida's words – was a kind of death sentence. Indeed, radical singularity is a state the poet will explore repeatedly throughout *Inferno*. It is Hell.

Dante's most radiant portrayal of civic life was his ancestor Cacciaguida's recollection of the commune in the good old days of the eleventh century: "Florence within her ancient ring of walls . . . sober and chaste, lived in tranquility" (*Par.* 15.97–9). Yet experience had taught him that the single city state, looking after its own self-interests and forever at odds with its neighbors, was a recipe for ongoing disaster. The old dream of a Holy Roman Empire was rapidly fading; nonetheless, it held out hope for a political structure less selfish and disposed to violence, more directed to unity and common cause. Looking north, he found in Henry VII of Luxembourg someone to believe in and a cause to support, especially as his exile gave him little reason to expect from the city state anything other than cause for despair.[6]

Dante characterized his exile as the experience of being lost at sea. "Truly," he wrote, roughly five years after leaving Florence, "I have been a ship without a sail and without a rudder, cast about to different harbors and inlets and shores by the dry wind of wretched poverty" (*Conv.* 1.3). He was a man without a country, as much beggar as pilgrim. Nautical images would later work their way into the *Commedia*, which begins in *Inferno* with the pilgrim likened to one escaped from a shipwreck at sea only to look back at the perilous waters he has somehow survived. In *Purgatorio* and *Paradiso* Dante goes on to liken himself to a mariner (and his poem to a boat), who ultimately finds port in Heaven's harbor. The struggle of the exile, however, would be to transform the shipwrecked man into the triumphant navigator. He will be a new Jason (*Par.* 33.94–6) who not only sails over previously uncharted seas but manages against all odds to obtain the Golden Fleece – in this case, the *Commedia* itself.

Dante effected this transformation in stages, all the while tasting the saltiness of unfamiliar bread and climbing borrowed staircases in other peoples' houses. He discovered that writing was a way to compensate for his losses – and writing well the best revenge. He earned his living by making his verbal skills valuable to one noble host or another. But he could also capitalize on his uprooting from the hubbub of Florence to free himself from the demands of civic and family life. Tragedy had given him an opportunity to develop his thoughts into an impressive body of prose.

On Vernacular Eloquence and Philosophy for All

Perhaps as early as 1303, Dante took advantage of being "one for whom the world is fatherland as the sea is for fish" (*De vulgari* 1.6). In *De vulgari eloquentia*, he wrote a thesis on the current state of the vernacular and on the possibility of finding true eloquence not only in Latin, where everyone expected to find it, but in Provençal, French, and Italian. His advocacy of the mother tongue, commonly considered to be inherently inferior, was written in the superior language of Church, University, and Empire: he made his case for the vernacular in Latin. With a confidence that characterizes everything he writes, he surveys the existing dialects and finds each of them wanting. Along the way he issues gold stars and demerits to the poets of his day, and in the process creates a place for himself to shine and for his own version of the Florentine dialect to take center stage.

The *De vulgari* begins with a history of language from Eden to the present day; in its second book it discusses the legitimate subjects of serious literature (war, love, and righteousness). It also gives guidelines for style, and makes magisterial judgments about which words are to be considered inappropriate for worthy poets to use – a list of prescriptions Dante later feels quite free to violate in the *Commedia*. Whatever Dante imagined the treatise would be when completed, the *De vulgari* breaks off in mid-sentence in its second book. Either the project ran out of steam or he decided that the way to demonstrate the power of the vernacular was to write it very well.

Between 1304 and 1307, he turned to another project, the *Convivio* or "Banquet." This work also stops before it is finished. Its introduction promises to make the High Table affair of philosophy accessible (this time in Italian) to the many vernacular "illiterates" who cannot read Latin. Fourteen books were meant to follow, each one centered on a multi-stanza poem – a *canzone* – which would in turn provide a springboard for various kinds of analysis. As in the *Vita Nuova*, the author interprets his own poetry in prose commentary. He displays his vernacular eloquence in both linguistic modes, shining as lyric poet, philosopher, and literary critic.

But if the *Convivio* in its "prosimetric" joining of prose and poetry looks back to Dante's meditation on his experience of Beatrice, the new work also entails a sharp break with the past. In its first book, the anonymous "gentle lady," who in the *Vita Nuova* offers the bereaved Dante consolation after the death of his beloved, is allegorized as Philosophy. In fact, as Dante says in an autobiographical aside, after the death of Beatrice he took up the study of philosophy (Boethius and Cicero) during a 30-month period of mourning. It was then that he frequented the monastic "schools of the religious" established in Florence by the Franciscans, Dominicans, and Augustinians.[7]

This study led him to a change of mind and heart: seasoned by grief, he would put away childish things and leave Beatrice for Lady Philosophy. The puerile romance of the *Vita Nuova* would become the serious business of what it means to *know*. Following the hard road of reason, it was possible to come to the philosopher's feast. Indeed, Dante would prepare a banquet open to "princes, barons, knights, and many other noble folk" along with clerics and scholars, and to "women no less than men, a vast number of both sexes, whose language is not that acquired through education, but the vernacular [volgari, e non literati]" (*Conv.* 1.9).[8] Philosophy was God's gift and by pursuing it a person could attain faith, hope, and charity – could reach a "celestial Athens" (*Conv.* 3.14).

One could also, as *Convivio* 4 demonstrates by repeated reference to Virgil's *Aeneid*, learn much about virtuous living by turning to the classics. In the first place, virtue should not be thought of as having to do with ancestry or handed down from generation to generation like the family silver. Rather it is the achievement of the earnest individual – the most adept readers of the *Convivio*, say, or the noble but not nobly born Dante. Aristotle is invoked first of all, but so too are Cicero and Virgil, Solomon and Boethius. The same imperial Rome that Augustine (d. 430) campaigned against so ferociously in his *City of God Against the Pagans* also became an ideal *Romanitas* to emulate. The student of philosophy had much to learn from the empire of Augustus, which was the universal authority God chose to pacify the world in preparation for the Incarnation of Christ. Indeed, Rome is part of a providential plan, and the extraordinary deeds of her great citizens were "not done without some light from the divine goodness over and above their natural goodness" (*Conv.* 1.4).

Universal Empire

Dante continued thinking about Rome and the virtues of empire in a later work, *Monarchia*, written some time between 1309 and 1313. It was at time when he was also busy with the *Commedia*. Likening himself to Daniel in the lion's den or singly facing off against a pagan ruler, he confronts the papacy and those who supported its temporal claims. He argues for an imperial government that would restore peaceful order to an Italy torn apart by factionalism. The Emperor has a God-given role to play and the earthly city a "beatitude" of its own that could flourish if spared some sword-wielding pope who had abandoned his pastoral staff. Let the Church lead people to life hereafter and the emperor, duly instructed by the pope in things eternal, enable them to live at peace in the here and now. Dante had hoped that Henry VII of Luxembourg would be this figure, but Florentine resistance to imperial claims and

Henry's early death prevented the dream from coming true after 1313. Nonetheless, it remained a dream.

Not surprisingly, the *Monarchia*, written in Latin and therefore certain to come to the attention of the authorities, was publicly burned in 1329. It was put on the Counter-Reformation's Index of Prohibited Books and kept there until 1921, when Benedict XV declared that, on the contrary, it articulated the *proper* relationship between Church and state.[9] The Pontiff was perhaps reflecting the "concordat" that the Vatican would enter into with a Fascist government. Benito Mussolini, who was said to read a canto of the *Commedia* every night before sleep, also loved the proimperial *Monarchia*, with its mysterious call for a DVX (*Purg.* 33.43), a leader sent from God who would redeem an Italy otherwise hopelessly divided.

The Birth of the Commedia

During the first decade of his exile from Florence, Dante was extraordinarily productive as a poet, literary critic, philosopher, and political thinker. His two works dating from this period, however, remain incomplete. Was this because he lost heart in attempting to carry out these grand projects or because something else, some new endeavor, claimed his attention? It is impossible to answer this question definitively, but easy to see the *Commedia* as a reprise of his previous works, which are deployed and often quite dramatically reworked within its three canticles and one hundred cantos. The poem's encyclopedic scope embraces almost every topic of discourse that Dante had thus far engaged – poetry and prose, literary history and theory, philosophy and political science – and always relates such objective concerns to the subjective realities of his own life.

Yet far more impressive than the poem's continuity with the past is a sense of *novità*, of the new, that emerges in the *Commedia*. Instead of writing primarily in prose, with sonnets or canzoni worked into a narrative framework, Dante gives us a sustained narrative poem, in which the poet's singular voice constantly gives way to the speech of others. Although it makes brief forays into other languages (Latin, Greek, Hebrew, and Provençal), by the poet's death in 1321 its more than 14,000 lines constituted the most extended example of Italian poetry. The distinctive *terza rima* rhyme scheme (aba, bcb, cdc) that propels the narrative forward is Dante's invention. No verse form moves so wonderfully, says poet James Merrill: ''Each tercet's first and third line rhyme with the middle one of the preceding set and enclose the new rhyme-sound of the next, the way a scull outstrips the twin, already dissolving oar-strokes that propel it'' (*PD*, p. 229). Also innovative are the *Commedia*'s wide mixture of styles, plenitude of distinct voices, and omnivorous appetite for virtually the whole of human experience (both sacred and secular). Then there is the architectural design of the entire work, whether detected on the minute level of end rhymes or in the broader reach of recurring themes and motives. Despite deep connections to the past, the *Commedia* is truly something new under the sun.

Vision or Brainstorm?

It was some time after 1308 that Dante began work on what would be his taskmaster for the rest of his life. We can only guess the poem's genesis. Perhaps it represented the deliberate resolution of a life crisis, an allegorical account of his rediscovery of Beatrice, his new appreciation of the writing of Virgil, and his personal synthesis of everything he had read and thought thus far. But surely its origins were more spectacular than any premeditated decision about "what to write next."

Did Dante have a brainstorm and "see the light" in a visionary explosion of imagination? Or was there some kind of rapture like the prophet Ezekiel's: "And the likeness of a hand was put forth and took me by a lock of my head: and the spirit lifted me up between the earth and heaven, and brought me in the vision of God into Jerusalem" (Ezek. 8:3)?[10] The author of the *Commedia* wanted his readers to believe something like this, to think that, like Ezekiel in the Old Testament or John the Divine in the New, he had been raised up by the hand of God, and received Heaven's commission to tell what he'd seen and heard. Even without giving credence to such rapture, one can see the poem as an extended prophetic "call" narrative in which the poet, like his scriptural predecessors in both testaments, is told to compose a divine message in his own words – in his case not in Hebrew, Greek, or Latin but in Italian.

Dante wrote when divine visions were by no means unusual. Indeed, a claim of spiritual illumination was often used by lay people to authorize their otherwise disregarded speech. No doubt some of Dante's contemporaries, like the credulous ladies of Verona mentioned by Boccaccio in his *Trattatello*, took the poet literally. Observing the somber Florentine making his way, they supposed that his grave mien and dark complexion were the result of time spent in "the heat and smoke down there." "Do you see the man who goes down to Hell, and comes again at his pleasure, and brings tidings of them that be below?" (*DCH*, p. 163). Reputedly, they would cross to the other side of the street when the poet came along.

The earliest commentators, such as Dante's son Pietro, were at pains to maintain a skeptical distance from such literalism. According to them, the poet was speaking metaphorically, as poets do, and was therefore only feigning the journey. When his father says that he descended into Hell, clarified Pietro, "he means that he descended mentally in imagination and not physically" (*DCH*, p. 136). Others finessed the issue and concentrated on the ultimate source of Dante's vision – God. According to Guido da Pisa, Dante was another prophet Isaiah, another Psalmist David: "for he was indeed the pen of the Holy Spirit, with which the Holy Spirit wrote speedily for us both the penalties of the damned and the glory of the blessed" (*DCH*, p. 127).

Textual Inspiration for the Poem

Perhaps fantasy can get us closer to the origins of the *Commedia* than anything else. Imagine it this way. Years into an exile that Dante has realized may never end, he paces the precincts of somebody else's garden. He is in a state of intense turmoil not only over his larger reversal of fortune but more specifically over his inability to bring to fruition the two works he had been laboring over. Suddenly – it is not clear whether the sound is in his own head or comes from the house next door – he hears a voice singing the same words over and over again: "Take it and read, take it and read." Remembering Augustine's famous garden moment in Milan he decides that whatever these strange words may mean, they are meant for him: a command to be taken literally. Again like Augustine, he rushes to retrieve the book he had distractedly set aside some time earlier, thinking that it might lead him through his present impasse and on to the great work he's meant to do.

And what might that book have been? Given Virgil's prominence in the *Commedia*, both as a guide throughout two-thirds of the journey and as an unmistakable subtext for the whole work, many have assumed that the *Aeneid* (with its hero's descent to the realm of the dead) is the "missing link" between *De vulgari* and *Convivio* and his poem. At least one scholar argued that Dante's impassioned reflection on the *Aeneid* in *Convivio* 4 primed him "to go himself, as a poet, to Hell and Heaven." [11]

For those looking for a "smoking gun," there are other possibilities. Might it be Augustine's *Confessions* that inspired Dante's imagination, with its exploration of an author's double identity – the past self and the present, who records a tale of transformation? A good case could be made as well for the poet's rediscovery of the *Vita Nuova* and therefore of Beatrice. Was it time to make good on the promise that ends his youthful *libello* "to compose concerning her what has never been written in rhyme of any woman"? Nor should we pass over the many accounts of visions or voyages to the afterlife that date from the third century to the thirteenth. This popular genre – *St. Patrick's Purgatory*, for instance, or the Visions of Thurkill and of Tundale – was much out of fashion by the time Dante turned to the *Commedia*. He might have determined to revive it, however, grafting its low-brow medieval sensibility onto the epic high culture of the classical *Aeneid*. Then again, he may have found in the Latin translation of the Arabic *Book of the Ladder* an account of Muhammed's night journey to Heaven and Hell that he could in his turn use for his known purposes – an "infidel" text to work along with all the other sources that produced the *Commedia*.

Finally, there's a chance that Dante took up and read a book he had always known but never before experienced at such a depth – God's Book, the Bible. Not that there would necessarily have been a single passage to inspire his future course, as was the case with Augustine, when a verse from Paul's Epistle to the Romans changed his entire life. Instead, the *Commedia* takes shape around the entire biblical canon. Christ's descent into Hell and resurrection on the third day makes possible

Dante's own story of redemption. Israel's exodus out of Egypt transfigures the tragedy of his exile into deliverance. Paul's rapture to the "third heaven" (2 Cor. 12:2) provides a precedent for his own vision and "apostolate." In this light, the poem may not only be his personal letter to the world – in which accounts would be settled, rough places made plain, the mighty brought low – but also, despite the wild audacity of the move, a third and newer Testament.

Once undertaken, the writing of the *Commedia* consumed the rest of Dante's life. Whatever he did in addition to this work, including *Monarchia* and a Latin lecture on geology (*Questio de aqua et terra*, 1320), did not interrupt the flow of cantos. We assume they came forth one after the other, in elaborate cross-referencing, and according to whatever master plan the poet *must* have had in mind from the beginning.

The Florentine chronicler Villani reports Dante to have been a scholar gypsy, first in the university "at Bologna, and afterwards at Paris, and in many parts of the world" (*DCH*, p. 149); there is also an English legend about an Oxford visit no doubt intended to counter the French connection. At Verona or Ravenna there would be letters (in Latin) to write for his host, personal favors to carry out, conversations to join, intellectual entertainment to provide.

There were also his own Latin epistles to compose – his dogged attempts, no matter how disenfranchised and beside the point he may have been, to sway the course of history. Thus he urges the Italian cardinals in Avignon's "Babylonian Captivity" to bring the seat of the Church back to Rome, and, in astonishingly biblical language, charges Henry VII of Luxembourg to fulfill his divine calling as Holy Roman Emperor by taking Florence by storm: "Behold now is the accepted time." The originals of these letters were apparently beautiful to behold. Although there is no extant record of Dante's penmanship, Leonardo Bruni in the fifteenth century noted that "his handwriting was perfect, and his letters were slender, long and very accurate."[12] Toward the end of his life there was also a poetic exchange in Latin with an admiring but disgruntled Bolognese scholar, Giovanni del Virgilio, who took Dante severely to task for wasting his great talent on the paltry vernacular.

Given the monumental weightiness of the *Commedia* – its massive architecture, density of reference and allusion, and mind-boggling coherence – the actual process of writing the text seems no less mysterious than its origins. We know nothing of Dante's personal library or how he might have had access to the myriad works he cites.[13] No doubt his memory was prodigious, as well as his ability to compose in his head, without resort to the endless "vision and revisions" made possible for us by computers and cheap paper. Moving from place to place, beholden to the generosity and whims of other people, it is difficult to conceive how he managed to sustain so complex a project for almost two decades, a work that never relents and seldom slacks off, that only grows in power.

Early Circulation of the Poem

After Guttenberg's invention of moveable type, the *Commedia* first appeared in print (and from three different presses) in 1472. Dante himself, however, belonged to the earlier manuscript era of book production and therefore released his text in installments during his own lifetime.[14] In this way he was "present" in Florence despite his actual absence from the city. Yet it was Bologna, with its venerable university and population of learned men, that was the earliest center of Dante "diffusion."

Boccaccio says that the poet made his work available to copyists in fascicles or *quadernetti,* little unbound booklets of between six to eight cantos. According to John Ahern, a scholar who has done much to help us understand the material production of the *Commedia*, Dante seems to have circulated installments of his work so as to achieve a rapid, economical reproduction:

> Although friends and family may have assisted him in producing such copies, given his relative poverty and isolation from major centers of book production, it is likely that he himself produced most of the copies that he sent out – on parchment (not paper) and in a double column format that would present, on two sides of a page, an entire canto.[15]

By late 1314, the whole of the *Inferno* was available; by autumn of 1315, the *Purgatorio*. The *Paradiso* was only just finished at the time of Dante's death in 1321, and most probably the first complete, bound edition of all hundred cantos was either the one made immediately by the poet's sons or the volume they sent to Dante's last patron, the lord of Ravenna, in 1322. Bound copies of the entire *Commedia* would have been very expensive and therefore quite rare. For this reason, the extraordinarily large number of early fourteenth-century book manuscripts that survive – 827, by one count – were most likely the work of enthusiastic readers who copied successive *quadernetti* for themselves.[16]

The *Commedia* was an immediate hit, and not only among the 7 percent of the total population who were the *literati*. These would have included judges, notaries, lawyers, civic administrators, doctors, and upper-level teachers; yet we also have indications that merchants (without much formal schooling) not only knew the poem but could quote from it.[17] So too the Italian Jewish community: from Emmanuel of Rome we have a sonnet on Dante's death and a Hebrew account, the *Mabberet ha-Tofet weha-Eden*, that tells of a journey through Hell and Paradise revealing the strong influence of the *Commedia*.

It was to assist this diverse group of readers that the commentary tradition came into being, starting almost immediately after the poet's death with his sons, Jacopo and Pietro. More skillful interpreters were quick to join in on the task of explication, to shed light on the poem's amalgam of philosophical and religious tradition, politics and literature. They were also keen to defend Dante's decision to write a narrative poem aimed toward the widest possible audience. And popular it was. Interest in the *Commedia* transcended the boundaries separating Guelph and Ghibelline, laypeople and clergy, those with impressive education and those with little at all.

Not that everyone was pleased with Dante's appeal to what turned out to be a mass audience. Giovanni del Virgilio, his sometime correspondent, was particularly fierce in this regard. Why should Dante waste his talent on a lay (or popular) song – *carmine laico* – written in a vulgar language that had thousands of idioms but no standards? It certainly had no credibility among the learned (like del Virgilio) who believed that Latinists should be the *Commedia*'s intended audience because they alone were sufficiently erudite to meet its demands. In the opening volley of a poetic debate he carried on with Dante he implores, ''Cast not in prodigality thy pearls before the swine, or load the Muses with garb unworthy of them'' (*DCH*, p. 106).

Dante's response might well have been that he wanted a much larger audience than the *literati* could provide. He hoped his work would touch the blacksmiths and donkey-drivers, fishwives and merchants who might come to know the *Commedia* second-hand. It did not matter that they could not actually read the text; after all, poems were songs – cantos and *canzoni* – meant to be sung or performed in dramatic recitation. Such delivery is precisely what we see in *Purgatorio*

2, for instance, when Casella takes the stage. Singing a poem from *Convivio* 3, "Amor che ne la mente mi ragiona" ("Love that discourses to me in my mind"), he enchants the newly arrived penitents at the base of Mount Purgatory not only with Dante's words but no doubt with his own mesmerizing rendition.

By contrast, the poet Petrarch complained to Boccaccio about how the "unskilled tongues of [Dante's] admirers defiled the poem" when they sang or declaimed it. Observing how familiar the ignorant marketplace masses (*idiotae*) were with Dante, Petrarch proclaimed himself free of any personal envy at his distinguished predecessor's success with the crowd. He dismisses "the applause and hoarse murmuring of dyers, drapers, shopkeepers, thugs, and their ilk" (*DCH*, p. 156). Such disdain seems like high-brow contempt for the medieval equivalent of a best seller.

The public was of a different mind. In 1373, Florentines of all sorts and conditions asked for a public reading of the poem to be followed by detailed commentary. They obviously wanted to applaud it all the more and knew they needed help. The commune complied with their wishes and Boccaccio was the obvious choice for the task. Many of the stories in his renowned vernacular collection, the *Decameron*, owed their origins to characters and episodes that first appeared in the *Commedia*. Furthermore, he had written his biography of the poet and even put together an anthology of his poetry. By popular demand, therefore, Boccaccio began a cycle of performance and exegesis of the poem at the church of San Stefano di Badia. Although he covered only about half of the *Inferno*, his effort became an institution.

Thus began the *lectura Dantis* tradition that continues till this day, not only in Florence and other cities in Italy but indeed throughout the world. In New England, for instance, there are several long-standing groups, usually led by local academics, now working their way through *Purgatorio* and *Paradiso*. According to the website of San Francisco's venerable Shrine Church of Saint Francis (http://www.shrinesf.org/lecturadantis.htm), "The *Lectura Dantis* group meets Wednesday evenings at 7:30 PM in the basement of the church for informal discussion. There are no formal writing assignments or tests. Anyone is welcome."

Not everyone acclaimed the poet as "divine." Some clerics thundered from their pulpits against his flights of fancy. The Dominican Guido Vernani went so far as to condemn Dante as a "vessel of the Devil" and "a man who wrote many fantastic things in poetry, a verbose solipsist [who] fraudulently seduces not only sickly minds but even zealous ones to the distraction of salutary truth" (*DE*, p. 855). The *Commedia*'s vivid presentation of the life to come apparently threatened to supersede authorized versions of the same. Certainly few in ecclesiastical authority would take kindly to Dante's withering portrayal of the Church and its hierarchy.

It is significant nonetheless that the first public exposition of the *Commedia* took place in a church. In its day, the poem was the only vernacular work to be given the kind of commentary treatment otherwise reserved for the Bible and such "canonical" classical authors as Virgil. It was second only to the Bible in its fourteenth-century proliferation, as we can tell by the number of early extant manuscripts and the sheer volume of *Commedia* citations in other works. Many of these manuscripts, like the printed editions that soon followed them, are gorgeously illustrated and embellished; others, like the 1502 "portable Dante," presented the printed text in a format similar to the compact, one-volume Bible produced in Paris in the early thirteenth century and used throughout Europe by students and preachers alike. By the mid-sixteenth century these associations with Holy Writ became official. In 1555, the one-word title that Dante gave to his poem, *Commedia*, was emended with the adjective "Divina." Ever since it has been customary to refer to the poem as the *Divine Comedy*. No doubt the poet would be very pleased.

How did Dante persevere with a project that, by his own account, made him "lean through these long years" (*Par.* 25.3)? In addition to returning his readers to the true way, he would write a vernacular poem so astonishing that it leaves all others, even the *Aeneid*, in the dust. His "song of myself" would make the fame-bedazzled Ovid, another of his ancient models, seem a shrinking violet. He also wrote a poem that he believed had a divine mission to reform the world and transform the reader. It is not necessary to *believe* Dante's claims, of course, when reading his work. He can be enjoyed entirely as a word magician without being heeded as a prophet. Yet no one remains unchanged by an encounter with the *Commedia*. It gets under the skin, into the blood, like few other texts. There are consequences to picking it up. Let the reader beware.

Chapter 2

Dante's Journey to God

A journey-taker is well advised to set off with a map in hand; so too a reader of Dante's *Commedia*. Before giving an interpretive retelling of the narrative in this chapter, it makes sense to sketch the imaginative world in which the poem takes place – a world the poet both received from his culture and made from scratch.[1] Because in the early fourteenth century both Hell and Purgatory could still be treated as actual terrestrial sites, Dante was able to show much of the hereafter as occupying the topography of the here and now. He could situate his exploration of the life to come in inaccessible regions of *this* life. For all but the final stage of his journey, therefore, the pilgrim travels through territory that, if off-limits to flesh and blood, could nonetheless be charted in the material heavens or located on an earthly map.

The general picture holds few surprises (see Figure 3). As might be expected for a medieval writer, it is composed from classical and Christian authorities rather than from observation. Dante views the earth as a ball largely covered by ocean, which he refers to in *Paradiso* 9.84 as "the sea that girds the world." The

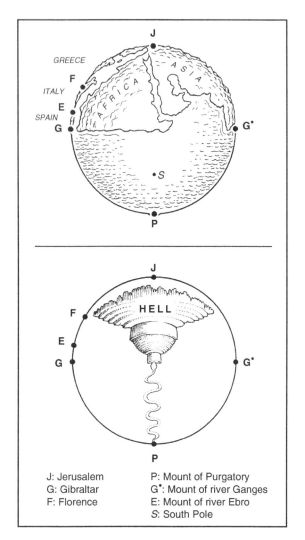

Figure 3 ''The Relative Positions of Gibraltar, Jerusalem, the Ganges, and Purgatory''
Courtesy of Robert Henry Turner

dry land surrounded by water is restricted to the Northern Hemisphere. This habitable earth extends from the western Pillars of Hercules (the Straits of Gibraltar) to the Indian river Ganges in the East; at its exact center stands Jerusalem. The Southern Hemisphere, at the antipodes, is a vast expanse of ocean. Although Dante was well aware of a diversity of opinion on the possibility of mortal life in the region, he follows St Augustine in rejecting it outright.

The *Commedia* assumes this understanding of the world's map and then changes it radically when Dante "discovers" in the supposedly vacant waters of the Southern Hemisphere a solitary landmass, a small island, located at the antipodes from Jerusalem's Mount Zion. From its shores rises a mountain of almost incalculable height. A stretch of the imagination is required to consider what effect this would have had on Dante's first readers, for in the *Commedia* he resolves not only the vexed question of Eden's whereabouts – most contemporaries thought of it as somewhere far in the East – but also the much-debated location of Purgatory. With the confidence of a traveler who has seen it all for himself, he shows that both sites occupy the same mountain, the one atop the other, and precisely on the other side of the globe from the holy city where Christ suffered his death. Single-handedly, he removed Eden to the Southern Hemisphere; he also brought Purgatory up from the horrors of the underworld and delivered it into the bright light of day. No one had ever joined these two locations so concretely or described them in such unforgettable detail. Nor had anyone else imagined their shared origin as Dante does in *Inferno* 34.

We learn that Satan, expelled from Heaven for refusing to worship God, plummeted to earth, plunged through its surface at the Antarctic pole, and buried himself at the dead center of the earth. In that tumble from spirit to flesh, he became the grotesque nightmare we know from medieval art. Upon impact, the dry land that once covered the Southern Hemisphere fled to the North. The land at the core of the earth shrank from Satan's presence, creating the pit of Hell surrounding his giant body; it also thrust upward into the watery expanse at the southern pole – like an erupting volcano. The result was a mountain "rising highest from the sea" (*Par*. 26.139). With Eden planted at its peak, it became the birthplace of humanity, and after Adam and Eve's sin, an uninhabited world forbidden to mortals. After the redemption of Christ, however, its steep slopes and garden summit again took on life. Flesh and blood were not permitted to return there; instead, the mountain would be a Purgatory where the penitent souls of the dead might work their way up its slopes, expiate their sins, and be born again into virtue.[2] By first drinking of Eden's river Lethe (which Dante took from Virgil's *Aeneid* 6) and then by immersion in the waters of Eunoe (a stream that flows entirely out of the poet's imagination), the penitents forget the bad and remember the good. From this earthly paradise, they make their way to the heavenly.

The true destination of the pilgrim's journey, as for any Christian Everyman, is the heavenly Jerusalem or, as Beatrice names it in *Purgatorio* 32, "the Rome where Christ is / Roman" (v. 102). Dante believed the City of God was located in the Empyrean, the 10th heaven of the Ptolemaic universe, which was wholly beyond the reach of time and space. The pilgrim journeys to the Empyrean by gradually ascending the nine material heavens, which are interlocking crystalline spheres holding the known planets and stars: the Moon, Mercury, Venus, the Sun, Mars, Jupiter, Saturn, and the Fixed Stars. Sweeping all along was the Primum Mobile, the ninth heaven, the outermost "skin" of the material world. At the core of this concentric universe stood the immobile earth. Around it danced the nine spheres, each one overseen by a different order of angels, each whirling at a different speed – all orchestrated into a cosmic dance.

In order to prepare the pilgrim for his vision of God "face to face" – that is, in order to share with him the beatific vision of the Trinity – the blessed appear in the successive material spheres. We see them either as individual flames or as constellations of light in various symbolic formations. Once Dante arrives in the Empyrean, however, he beholds them in the bodies they will have at the end of time, after the General Resurrection of the Dead.[3] They sit in the round, higher or lower depending on their spiritual "size place" and in demonstration of the hierarchy that Dante believed to be fundamental to existence. Arranged within a structure "in the shape of [a] white rose" (*Par.* 31.1), they contemplate God, love him to the capacity of their vision, and shine with corresponding ardor. It is at the golden center of this "rosa sempiterna" (*Par.* 30.124) that the pilgrim joins the blessed in their contemplation of the Triune God. With that vision, which Dante finally cannot describe, the journey ends, the pilgrim becomes the poet, and the writing of the *Commedia* begins.

Inferno

The poem opens with Dante looking back to a time when he, the pilgrim, was lost. His name isn't given here, and indeed is disclosed two-thirds of the way through the journey and then only once (*Purg.* 30.55). Nor are we told anything about his identity apart from his age when the disaster took place. He was 35, "in the middle of the journey of our life" (*Inf.* 1.1), according to the Bible's calculation of a lifespan as threescore years and ten (Ps. 90:10, Douay 89:10). Anything else about him as a character is superfluous: what matters is his survival in a "dark wood" that is many things at once: wilderness and sea, labyrinth with no exit, a void that threatens to swallow him whole.

Literary resonance within these opening lines connects this shadowy landscape to other texts, for this new account in the Florentine vernacular has ancient Latin antecedents as venerable as Virgil's *Aeneid*, the *Confessions* of Augustine, and the Bible. Yet what is highlighted is not literary history but the terror of the present moment of writing. If, through memory, the poet re-enters the nightmare that once almost destroyed him, will he survive?

The recollected story begins in twilight. Along with the pilgrim who comes to himself in the "selva oscura" we readers are also in a dreamscape. Apparently concrete elements (a high mountain, the bright sun, and the three beasts that shortly prevent his escape) seem to mean something beyond what they denote – but what? The narrative unfolds in the realm of allegory, where a single action or entity can contain several senses or levels of meaning, and carry multiple associations. A desperate man aspires to move toward the light without the poet needing to spell out "enlightenment" or "salvation" as the pilgrim's goal. The beasts are another matter: the reader wants to know what they are. Yet much as Dante's commentators from the very beginning have wanted to determine what the lion, leopard, and she-wolf mean – sinful dispositions is a good guess – the poet keeps them only an indeterminate menace. They may represent forces that are inside the would-be climber *and* that exist in the world outside him: pride, envy, wrath, the rapacious desire for more.

Then someone appears in the void. He is a ghost, a man, a human voice at the very least – someone to whom the desperate man pleads for mercy in words that echo Psalm 51:1, "*Miserere* di me!" (Douay, Ps. 50:1), "Have mercy on me." This figure changes the whole mood of the story. We are no longer locked in a nightmare, a shadowy space that might as well be the speaker's psyche. Now, suddenly, we are in history and faced with someone who has specificity. He recalls his parents and birthplace, the political order under which he lived, the religion of his day, the great poem he wrote.

His appearance on the scene comes as a surprise, as it must have seemed to Dante's medieval readers encountering this text for the first time. For the Christian pilgrim wandering in the dark wood is rescued by none other than the ancient *pagan* poet Virgil (d. 19 BCE). Virgil wrote the *Aeneid* as well as sets of poems called *Eclogues* and *Georgics*; he also represented the best of the ancient world.[4] Not that he is only a general culture hero: Virgil, as we soon discover, is Dante's personal role model. Thus the pilgrim calls him ''[the] light and honor of all other poets'' (*Inf.* 1.82), ''the fountain / that freely pours so rich a stream of speech'' (1.79–80).

> You are my master and my author, you –
> the only one from whom my writing drew
> the noble style for which I have been honored.
> (*Inf.* 1.85–7)

Later we will learn that this rescue of the pilgrim took place for purposes greater than his personal salvation. He was saved in order to write a ''volume'' that would shed its own light, a poem that would offer a way to combat the three beasts and ascend the heights. For now, however, it is enough that Dante meets the first of several guides in the afterlife who help him along a pathway he could never navigate alone.

The way up is the way down

The pilgrim wants, quite naturally, to move upward, but the journey must first lead him down, away from the light, and into a succession of spiritual dark woods of which the opening "selva oscura" is but a shadowy forecast. This is a prospect so frightening that no sooner has Dante thrown in his lot with Virgil than he changes his mind. Who is *he*, anyway, to take on this journey? Not an ancient hero like Aeneas or a Christian apostle like Paul – no one foolish enough to risk the heart of darkness.

In the first of many interventions, Virgil assures him that he is not on his own: his journey to the depths turns out to have its warrant in the highest heaven. Three "blessed women" (2.124–5) – the Virgin Mary, St Lucy, and Dante's earthly beloved, Beatrice – have initiated his movement toward the light; they know it can only take place after an immersion in the dark. The pattern is biblical and sacramental. Just as Israel's Promised Land stands on the far shore of the Egyptian Red Sea; just as Christ descended *ad infernos* before he ascended into Heaven; and just as the "new life" of baptism emerges from the waters of sin and death, so an experience of the City of God requires a "crash course" in Hell.

Inferno 3–34 presents this descent gradually, through a succession of concentric cityscapes that mirror ancient Babel, Troy, and Thebes as well as the thirteenth-century city states of northern Italy: Venice and Siena, Lucca and Pistoia, Pisa and Genoa, and most bitterly, the poet's own Florence (see Figure 4). In canto after canto we move through gates and within walls, over bridges and around cemeteries. Sometimes Dante encounters figures he recognizes from history and literature, but more often he keeps company with near contemporaries, even with people he knows personally. He is aghast to discover souls in Hell he never expected to find there (the reverse will be true in *Purgatorio*). Most of them he treats with an affection and civility strangely out of place in the "dolorous kingdom."

The inscription above the Gates of Hell in *Inferno* 3 famously says, "ABANDON EVERY HOPE, WHO ENTER HERE" (l. 9); it goes on to proclaim that justice "moved" God to construct the eternal prison in the first place. From the threshold of Hell, therefore, the poet raises difficult questions about divine justice. Dante may well (like Milton after him) want to "justify the ways of God to men," but nonetheless makes his task in this regard very difficult. Villains and monsters pose little problem, at least if one entertains a notion of Hell as just deserts for wrong-doing. But what about the poignant lovebird Francesca (canto 5), the public-spirited Farinata and Cavalcanti (10), the courtly Pier della Vigna (13), the paternal Brunetto Latini (15), the eloquent Ulysses (26)? And what of those who, like Virgil himself, are said to have erred only in lacking baptism? It is impossible to dismiss these vivid, multidimensional characters merely as instances of vice or sin personified.

Nor does Dante's pilgrim do so. He swoons after listening to Francesca's romance, praises his old teacher Brunetto to the skies, and is so intent upon hearing the words of the golden-tongued Ulysses that he nearly falls into the ditch of the false counselors. It is largely the force of context – this is Hell, after all – and the warnings of Virgil to pay attention, that raise suspicions about the innocence of these characters and God's alleged injustice in damning them. Context, and close attention to the beguiling words they speak, "innocent" as they are of the truth about themselves.

The whole of the *Commedia* is based on the assumption that each individual chooses his or her place in the afterlife. Such a choice is the most important one anyone can make; it also goes into effect only after one's last breath. Until that moment, freedom of choice remains. At the end point, however, the choice is irrevocable. Dante is so fervent a believer in free will (which preoccupies *Purgatorio* 17, the central canto of the entire poem) that he presents the damned as actually desiring their ends. Indeed, they rush toward Minos, the judge of Hell, who discerns their deepest longing and sends them to their particular "reward." They are given for eternity what they most loved on earth; their punishment is a version of their *modus vivendi.*

The justice of this assignment is called "il contrapasso." The notion of sin being its own punishment prevails throughout *Inferno,* although it is only given a name in canto 28, and by one of the damned in the circle of the Sowers of Discord. As a result of separating a father from a son, a king from his heir apparent, and therefore a Provençal kingdom from itself, Bertran de Born spends eternity with his head severed from his trunk. His damnation exemplifies his sin: "in me," he says, "one sees the law of counter-penalty [il contrapasso]" (*Inf.* 28.141–2). Retrospectively, we discern *contrapasso* in the eternal storm of the lustful or the boiling pitch of those who in life were mired in crooked deal-making. The crime becomes the punishment.

Imagining the void

Where did Dante's vision of damnation come from? Virgil's Tartarus in *Aeneid* 6 gives one kind of blueprint. The City of Dis, which Virgil and the pilgrim enter with such difficulty in *Inferno* 9, is modeled on its massive wall and gates, its tower and threatening furies. Inside, Virgil places the dregs of society: fratricides, parent beaters, adulterers, traitors, and exploiters of the poor. Yet the damned of Tartarus are not singled out by name or arranged in any coherent order; nor is Aeneas allowed to pass through their midst as the pilgrim does throughout the circles of Hell. Aeneas hears about but does not see the damned.

Virgil's Tartarus no doubt influenced how Christian authors imagined Hell in the many dream visions and journeys to the afterlife that date from the mid-second century Apocalypse of Peter to the Visions of Tundale (1149), the Monk of Evesham (1196), and Thurkill (1206).[5] These works bring the reader to both Heaven and Hell, with only a rudimentary suggestion of Purgatory's middle space. Compared to the *Aeneid*, they show more interest in differentiating categories of the damned and in describing their often hideous punishments. Dante may have learned from these writers, and yet the contrast between their essentially crude narratives and *Inferno*'s psychological depth and sophisticated structural organization is more striking than any kinship.[6]

Unlike these afterlife visions, moreover, Dante presents us with geography and indeed with a cosmos thoroughly determined by theology. Space is never neutral or insignificant: everything seems to mean something. Yet the poet's gift for detailed observation is controlled by a mind informed by the Scholastic master's drive for order, conceptual clarity, and fine distinctions. Not to mention irony.

Take the figure of Satan, for instance. Frozen at earth's center stands transfixed the gigantic, repellent monster of medieval nightmare. Once Lucifer, angel of light, he became darkness visible through pride. This Emperor of Hell rules from the nadir, the base of the geocentric universe. Dante stresses not only Satan's gross size but the extent to which he is an elaborate travesty of things heavenly. His six, bat-like wings bespeak the hideous transformation of a seraph. His hairy flesh is a "take off" on the Incarnation, the three faces on his head a grotesque of the Trinity, his ceaseless chewing of three of the damned an inversion of Christ's Eucharistic self-offering, "Take, eat, this is my body given for you."

Guiding this extended parody is a notion Dante inherited from the theological tradition of Augustine and Aquinas, namely that evil has no positive nature but is only the loss or privation of good. When Lucifer "lifted his brow against his Maker" (*Inf*. 34.35) – or when, according to Augustine, he preferred to love himself rather than God – he lost his status as well as his beauty. He devolved into a bad joke, a "spoof" of the One he aspired to surpass.

If the notion of evil as privation of good inspired Dante to imagine Satan as a composite negation, it also controlled his construction of the entire *Inferno*. Just as Satan himself imitates God, Hell's nine concentric circles are a perverse imitation of the nine celestial spheres that spin about the divine still point we encounter at the end of *Paradiso*. Instead of moving upward, as Dante does in both *Purgatorio* and *Paradiso*, he moves steadily down in *Inferno* (and mostly in the "sinister" direction of left). Instead of plunging into "the mighty sea of being" (*Par.* 1.113), he takes step after step toward nothingness, falling into the spiritual equivalent of a black hole.

The *Commedia*'s journey culminates in the City of God, whose only boundaries are love and light (*Par.* 28.54). In the *Inferno*'s first installment, however, the poet posits the heavenly city's antithesis. Hell is constructed primarily out of allusions to the wrongdoings of the Italian towns Dante knew from birth and over the course of his exilic wanderings. *Inferno* presents our world without grace, our lust for power without mercy. We encounter what Augustine speaks of as *libido dominandi*, the lust for domination. Here the self is sovereign, frozen in obsessive monomania – always alone no matter how dense the crowd. In *Inferno* 10, for instance, Farinata and Cavalcanti, two men formerly united by citizenship, class, religion and their children's betrothal, occupy the same sarcophagus but have no contact with one another. Why? One is Ghibelline, the other Guelph. Dante speaks with each individually but never together. Despite the fact of their shared incarceration, they have "nothing" in common.

Dante's journey through *Inferno* engages his empathy from time to time by reminding him how often evil is a flawed good, a corrupted virtue. Yet by the time he comes to the frozen lake at the "base of all the universe" (*Inf.* 32.8), Hell is exposed as a

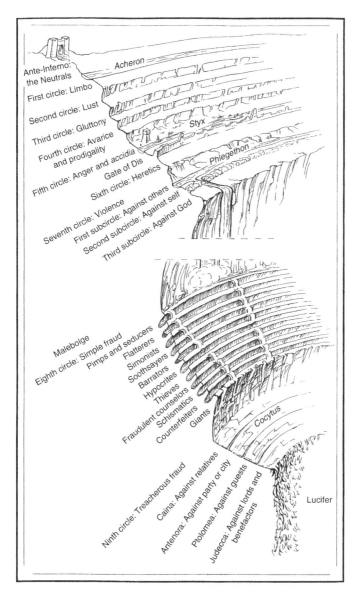

Figure 4 "The Structure of Dante's Hell"
Courtesy of Robert Henry Turner

place where the atrocities of earth rage for eternity. Only now horror is turned against those who once perpetuated it; victimizers become subject to their own evil. Thus the rivers of Hell, which collectively torment the damned, are revealed to have a common source on the earth: they begin as the *lacrimae rerum*, the tears of violated humanity (*Inf.* 14.112–20). What has gone around comes around – and lasts forever.

Bottom of the universe

Dante descends into Hell along the proverbially slippery slope where bad steadily leads to worst. Sins of the appetite are encountered first, and through them the corruption of the flesh, gathered into what we might think of as the outlying suburbs of the damned. Once inside the City of Dis (*Inf.* 10), Dante experiences the corruption of a higher human faculty, the will, as it turns in various ways toward violence (against God, against others, against one's own self). Another descent takes the pilgrim down to Malebolge (*Inf.* 18), a city within a city, where fraud provides examples of intelligence and ingenuity – *ingegno* or genius – that have been brought into the service of evil. Finally, Dante is lowered to the "bottom of the entire universe" (*Inf.* 32.8), where he finds the many permutations of treachery that erode human connection, whether to kin, those joined by covenant, guests, or a superior – in Satan's case, God. Cocytus is the *Commedia*'s concentration camp of purest evil, which the poet depicts as a realm not of fire, but of ice.

This is "the center to which all weight is drawn" (32.73–4). Or, to be more literal, the center to which every weight "si rauna" – "reunites itself," "makes itself one again." Any true notion of *e pluribus unum*, one out of many, is foreign to the spirit of Hell. Instead, we see the relentless desires of the radically private ego and the absolute refusal of partnership. Nonetheless, "si rauna" ironically sets the stage for what is perhaps Dante's most disturbing exposure of evil. It takes place in the company of traitors who broke faith with their political party. In this case, we have a count and an archbishop who represent corruption within the state as well as the Church. Before we learn any of these particularities, however, we see an enactment of the hatred that is their only connection:

> I saw two shades frozen in one hole
> so that one's head served as the other's cap;
>   and just as he who's hungry chews his bread,
> one sinner dug his teeth into the other
> right at the place where brain is joined to nape:
>   no differently had Tydaeus gnawed the temples
> of Menalippus, out of indignation,
> than this one chewed the skull and other parts.
>   "O you who show, with such a bestial sign,
> your hatred for the one on whom you feed,
> tell me the cause," I said; "we can agree
>   that if your quarrel with him is justified,
> then knowing who you are and what's his sin,
> I shall repay you yet on earth above,
>   if that with which I speak does not dry up."
>
> (*Inf.* 32: 125–39)

The poet sets the stage with a hideous visual effect. In a grotesque rendering of a back-to-front embrace – the "spoon" position – one man gnaws the skull of another. The precision of this description is elaborately gruesome. The two skulls are so close that "one's head served as the other's cap" and the placement of teeth on bone is "right at the place where brain is joined to nape." If you want to know the ferocity with which this attack is prosecuted, imagine a starving man confronting food. Several readings are necessary to get beyond the blood and gore, to see, for instance, that Dante is playing hideously with notions of unity. Two figures are frozen in one hole; one man's head is the other's hat; one man's teeth are fused with another man's skull ("and other parts"). This vision of dog-eat-dog is also the perversion of a Communion, with flesh becoming bread. The hatred is so deep that only cannibalism can suggest its fury.

Because Dante wants to understand who these figures are and what motivates such disfiguring hatred, he promises the avenger to share what he learns with the living – if, that is, his tongue does not dry up on the spot. With the possibility of a story perhaps too horrendous to tell, the next canto opens with another visual assault:

> That sinner raised his mouth from his fierce meal,
> then used the head that he had ripped apart
> in back: he wiped his lips upon its hair.
>   Then he began: "You want me to renew
> despairing pain that presses at my heart
> even as I think back, before I speak.
>   But if my words are seed from which the fruit
> is infamy for this betrayer whom
> I gnaw, you'll see me speak and weep at once."
> *(Inf.* 33.1–9)

"*La bocca.*" The initial word of the opening line in Italian is "mouth": it both gnaws *and* speaks, both eats this savage meal *and* delivers the dreadful words, the bestial signs, of the narrative to follow. The one who speaks wastes the head in front of him; then he wipes the filth from his mouth with his victim's hair. Horror. But Dante also presents the soul as a pathetic figure looking for pity. His memory is grief and his heart contracts when he thinks about the past (which, of course, is all he has). Above all, the one who gnaws and speaks has a mission: his narrative is meant to bear "the fruit of infamy," his purpose to destroy whatever remains on earth of "this betrayer whom I gnaw."

So be it. Cocytus is the region of treachery, and therefore the masticated traitor – who turns out to be an Archbishop of Pisa – is exactly where he belongs. Yet given Hell's unerring justice, the one who speaks of his just vengeance at such length is also in his proper place. Count Ugolino may be allowed to participate in the punishment of his "companion," Archbishop Ruggieri, but is nonetheless frozen in the same hole as the sinner he ravages. He plays the part of avenging angel, but this role turns out to be an aspect of his damnation. He can neither hate enough nor entirely consume his enemy.

For the reader who is aware that in "la nostra vita" justice often does *not* prevail, there may be something comforting in this assurance of retribution. Who would not want Satan (and everything he represents), frozen immobile and securely under divine control? Yet the closing cantos of *Inferno* are anything but comforting. Ugolino recounts how he and his altogether innocent sons were starved to death by Archbishop Ruggieri in a Pisan tower (subsequently named the Tower of Hunger) that was still standing in the poet's own day. In the second half of the same canto, Brother Alberigo not only reports that he had relatives murdered at his own table in the course of a meal – surely bad enough – but reveals a still worse possibility. A person can commit acts so heinous that, even before mortal death, the soul plummets to Hell while a demon continues to animate his or her body on earth. Such stories suggest that the membrane between Inferno and actual cities like Pisa or Genoa is distressingly porous. It is barely there at all.

Even if an ultimate reckoning awaits us at death or the end of time, these narratives in Cocytus remind us that on earth there is no *deus ex machina* to snatch Ugolino's children out of the Tower of Hunger's nightmare, or to prevent Brother Alberigo's guests from being murdered in cold blood at table. No divine intervention, no ram in the thicket to substitute for the human sacrifice – here there is, quite literally, no exit. When Christ descended to the dead after his crucifixion he may have put down Satan under his feet, but devils are nonetheless still at play on earth, fooling us in their human disguise.

The poet concludes his encounter with a reference to Pisa, the earthly city that both traitors shared. He denounces it as a "new Thebes," the shame of Italy, a canker. Since nearby towns are slow to punish their hateful neighbor, Dante takes it upon himself to invoke a catastrophe that will wipe the slate clean. Let two small islands suddenly block the river Arno and so flood the city of Pisa "that it may drown every soul in you!" (33.82–4).

God called for a flood at the beginning of human history "because [the earth] was corrupt in God's sight" (Gen. 6:11); Abraham interceded on behalf of Sodom and Gomorrah, convincing the Lord not to destroy the city if 10 just men could be found (Gen. 18). Dante, however, is not interested in mercy's half measures. He usurps the divine perspective (and the prerogative that goes with it), proposing to avenge the Pisan *innocenti* by drowning an entire population.

What do we make of this? Dante uses the Ugolino story to urge an end to violence and revenge. May no one ever again lose his children in the Tower of Hunger! Yet he calls for divine vengeance on Pisa, counting on his authority as a sacred poet who claims to be coauthoring a text with God.

Is an omniscient Dante staging this moment in order to show, through his own persona as poet, how difficult it is to withstand the impulse toward evil, especially for those in the business of righteous indignation? Or are we catching him with his guard down: an angry man embittered by his personal experience of the political process, who writes this lengthy poem about divine judgment in order to settle scores as he (and, of course, God) sees them? Such disfigurement may be what happens when the imagination plummets to the bowels of the universe. You take on the attributes of Lucifer, the angel of light who, even before Adam and Eve, wanted to be divine. You destroy one group of innocents in order to avenge another. It's dangerous to become a judge, much less a connoisseur of justice.

It is a great pity that *Inferno* is the only portion of the *Commedia* most people read, because the rest of the work serves to melt the *Inferno*'s deep freeze, to give a sense of hope. The poem is a journey, after all, and not a dead end. Certainly we need another view of the "divine" poet, whose own hatred and rage at injustice in *Inferno* 33 threaten a return to the dark wood rather than an escape from it. The second stage of the journey, *Purgatorio*, affords us just that view.

Purgatorio

We might well have arrived at the gates of Purgatory simply by the turn of a page. Instead, Dante makes us work for our approach to the second kingdom. At the very center of *Inferno*'s 34th canto, Dante and Virgil complete their descent into Hell by crawling along the hairy flank of the imprisoned Satan. Midway down his body they turn themselves around and start climbing upward, along a narrow passageway that will lead them (in 12 hours and just a few lines!) to the shores of an unimaginably high mountain, perhaps the one that Dante could not climb at the outset. Looking back from this new orientation, the pilgrim sees that Satan is absurdly upside down. From this perspective, we realize that everything in Hell is topsy-turvy. Or, using the analogy of photography, what we have seen thus far is a negative image that Purgatory will now "develop" into a true picture. Instead of continuing to dip his pen in darkness, the poet is now writing with light.

Light, in fact, is the first thing we notice in Purgatory. Dante's arrival is just before dawn, when the planet Venus makes the whole sapphire-hued east "smile." Through a chronology revealed only piecemeal in *Inferno*, we gradually realize the poem's time-frame. Dante descended into Hell on Good Friday of the year 1300; by the time he makes it to the shores of Purgatory's island mountain it is Easter morning. His pilgrimage, in other words, is aligned with the Savior's Passion, Death, and Resurrection. Dante moves in imitation of Christ.

From this first starry moment onward, his journey takes place (or bides its time) in the freshest air. The pilgrim's path will be illumined during the day by a sun that rises and sets in great beauty. When the sun is "silent," as it was menacingly in *Inferno* 1, there is brilliant recompense in luminous planets and constellations. Freed from the claustrophobia of Hell, we find ourselves not only newly risen from the grave but part of a cosmological pull toward the heavens that keeps drawing the penitents "up."

All of this would, as I suggested above, have immediately startled Dante's medieval readers, whose notion of Purgatory was subterranean, ghastly, and similar to Hell in its horrors save that one day its torments end. Theologians stayed clear of thinking too concretely (or speaking too conclusively) about Purgatory's whereabouts. It was enough to see it as an antechamber to Inferno, where the soul would pay off its debt of sin with agony and burn off the residue of evil. The penitent would serve an appropriate prison sentence, and then move on to his or her reward. The duration of this penal sentence depended upon the gravity of a person's sins as well as the extent that the living – by the "suffrages" of prayers or said masses – helped speed their loved ones along.

Dante accepted these basic theological premises but completely altered the atmosphere of Purgatory and the primacy traditionally given to suffering (see Figure 5). To begin, the "second kingdom" was not located underground; instead,

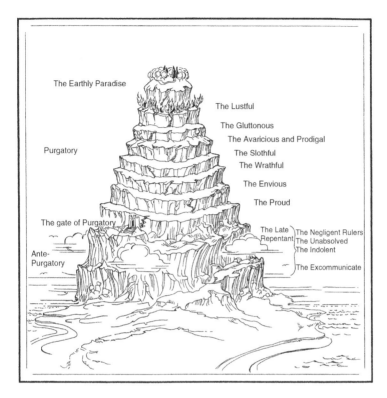

The Earthly Paradise

The Lustful

The Gluttonous

The Avaricious and Prodigal

Purgatory

The Slothful

The Wrathful

The Envious

The Proud

The gate of Purgatory

The Late Repentant
The Negligent Rulers
The Unabsolved
The Indolent

Ante-Purgatory

The Excommunicate

Figure 5 "The Structure of Purgatory"
Courtesy of Robert Henry Turner

it spiraled upward along the sides of the mountain. Its pathway moved from left to right, and therefore reversed the "sinister" leftward direction of Hell's descent. It was also divided into three discrete sections, the first of which, an Ante-Purgatory, seems to have been one of Dante's inventions. Here at the base of the mountain he gathers souls not yet ready to begin the hard climb. There are those who repented only in the last desperate moment of their lives; those who, through sloth, barely repented at all; and those who were so preoccupied with worldly governance that they neglected to prepare themselves for the life to come.

The seven terraces, each devoted to one of the deadly sins, constitute Purgatory proper. In every case, repentance of sin entails painful self-confrontation and arduous acts of contrition. It hurts the pilgrim even to look! Yet the mountain is hardly the grisly torture chamber commonly imagined in the Middle Ages. As Dante counsels his readers, the whole point of the process is not pain but gain: "Don't dwell upon the form of punishment," he says, "consider what comes after that" (*Purg.* 10.109–10).

The "after that" is the variety of penance we observe: heavy burdens borne by the proud (cantos 10–12), sewn-up eyes of the envious (13–14), or a corridor of purifying fire through which the lustful (equally represented by groups we would call heterosexuals and homosexuals) make their circuitous way (26). Seeing each penance enacted, we can readily imagine its termination. The proud will cast off their dead weights; the lustful will step out of the fire and into the garden that blooms, cool and green.

Because the end result of Purgatory is what matters, Dante shows us a realm of transformation that bears little resemblance to the traditional spiritual penitentiary. Rather, it is a hospital for the healing of brokenness; a school for the learning of truth; an incubator in which worms grow up to be butterflies; a conservatory where soloists become a chorus, and speakers develop a use for "we" and "us" in addition to "I" and "me." Life "sentences" are not served, they are rewritten.

Other analogies, both of them anachronistic, also spring to mind. Purgatory is a naturalization center in which immigrants become citizens of the City of God. Or, the whole experience of the Mountain of Purgatory can be likened to a psychoanalysis, where the analysand painfully unties the knots of the past so as to live more freely in an unencumbered future. Hell was all about repetition-compulsion, an endless replay of the sinner's "song of myself." Purgatory, on the contrary, is dynamic, dedicated to change and transformation. It concerns the rebirth of a self free at last to be interested in other souls and other things.

Inventing Purgatory

What differentiates those forever doomed to Inferno from those who get to work their way through Purgatory to Paradise? "Technical" answers to this question show Dante working within a received Catholic theological tradition at the same time that he alters it to suit his purpose. The damned consigned to Inferno include some virtuous pagans like Virgil who lacked Christian baptism and therefore were deprived of the gift of faith. Unbaptized infants officially fall into this category, whereas the pagan worthies we attend to in *Inferno* 4 were the poet's own invention.[7] (This liberty was roundly condemned at the time by the Dominicans in Florence, who forbade the *Inferno* to impressionable novices in the order.) With the exception of a few notoriously evil pagans taken from ancient history or literature, however, Hell is mostly populated by Italian Christians who, although baptized, were unrepentant at the time of their death. By Dante's lights, "Christendom" does not come off very well in God's judgment. This notion is reinforced when we learn in the heavenly rose that only half of the blessed will date from the Christian era; the rest are ancient Hebrews (*Par.* 32.37–9)

The souls we meet in Purgatory have not lived lives of particular virtue or faithfulness. They may even have delayed repentance until their last breath and managed no more than a "little tear" of genuine repentance. No matter how minimally, however, they turned to God before their end and therefore died in a state of grace. No matter how long it may take to transform a forgiven sinner into a saint, the redemption of each is secure.

At first, Hell-Purgatory's juxtaposition of damnation and salvation seems clear, if arbitrary. One senses (if not assents to) the theological rationale for who's "in" and who's "out," who is damned for eternity or passing through purgation on the way to Paradise. More than once Dante depicts members of the same family to heighten a distinction between the damned and the saved, to "show just cause" for one or the other's fate. In *Inferno* 27, for instance, we meet Guido da Montefeltro, whose ostensibly genuine conversion to a monastic life in his later years was in truth utterly hollow. His son Buonconte, by contrast, made no such show of piety so that the public record knew only of his sins. Yet when he died on the battlefield, girded by debris rather than dressed up and cinctured in a monk's robe, he freely gave himself up to repentance, his arms making the sign of the cross on his chest. Upon their deaths, a demon claimed the father, an angel the son. Learning the full story behind the deceptive appearances, the reader understands each fate. God alone knows the truth that counts.

But Dante proceeds to complicate theological matters, especially when it comes to those virtuous pagans whom he otherwise relegated to damnation. In the very first canto of *Purgatorio*, Dante and Virgil encounter the guardian of the mountain, Cato. This is quite a surprise for the one placed in charge of all new arrivals to Purgatory's shores. True, he is Moses-like, framed by stars, his face compared to the rising sun. Yet Cato was not only a pagan suicide, but an ardent enemy of Julius Caesar, and therefore of the imperial ideal Dante celebrates throughout the *Commedia*. Here he is!

Nor is Cato the only exception to this baptismal rule. In *Paradiso* 20 and in the context of open astonishment – "Who would believe it?'' (l. 67) – we find the soul of Ripheus, a very minor character from Virgil's pagan *Aeneid*, who appears in the Heaven of Divine Justice in the company of no less than King David, ancestor of Christ. With both Cato and Ripheus, or so it would seem, righteousness and a thirst for justice constituted a kind of sacrament. At least of Ripheus we are told, ''through grace on grace, God granted him / the sight of our redemption in the future'' (*Par.* 20.122–3). In Hell, the judgment of God seems to play by precise (if severe) rules; yet divine grace proves to be the wild card as the poem moves forward and loosens up.

What the souls in Purgatory have in common, no matter how ill-prepared they may have been at their time of death, is their final turn toward God. *Self*-involvement is essentially what Dante understands sin to be – a destructive narcissism whose impulse is to erase the Other to secure one's own ''divine right.'' Every compartment of Hell is full of fresh examples. In the course of moving through *Inferno*, moreover, we also see that solipsism is never a victimless crime. Rather, it is always social in its effect: a private kiss can bring down a kingdom; a single alchemist can debase a currency.

The opposite is true as well. We learn in *Purgatorio* that virtue can open up locked doors, can bring a new understanding of life that amounts to a reinvention of the status quo. Provenzan Salvani, Tuscany's most arrogant grandee, set up shop as a beggar in the Campo of Siena, ''to free / his friend from suffering in Charles's prison, / humbling himself, he trembled in every vein'' (11.136–8). What could have led such a person to ''set aside all shame'' and prize someone other than himself but love? Nor is love for the living the only one that matters. Those on earth can speed a soul on its way up the mountain by praying for the deceased. The pilgrim's popularity in Purgatory, seen most dramatically at the beginning of canto 5 when the souls nearly mob him, stems from the fact that he can enlist "prayer power," either through his own intercessions or by asking relatives to offer suffrages on their behalf.

The key to all of Purgatory is love. Virgil explains this at length at *Commedia*'s midpoint in *Purgatorio* 17–18. Along the seven terraces – set up sequentially to address pride, envy, wrath, sloth, avarice/prodigality, gluttony, and lust – the most grievous sins are clustered lower on the mountain, when alienation from love is most apparent. Arrogance is considered more deleterious than lust, for instance. Those sins closer to the top represent a mistaken or excessive desire, which once led souls to pursue a lesser good with the zeal that should have been reserved for God. Food was misused, creature comforts made too much of, sex pursued in ways that were unhealthy or compulsive. The journey up the Mountain of Purgatory, therefore, amounts to a proper reordering of love.

The program of the terraces

On each of the terraces, a particular failure in love is suffered, rectified, and transformed into a virtue that corresponds to the vice. The proud, for example, suffer the heavy burden of their egos, which are represented by the rock each one is bowed under. Their punishment is to carry this increasingly oppressive and false "persona" until they can willingly let go of it. When they are able to do so, they stand tall, at last free of what they mistakenly thought was their true self.

How quickly this liberation takes place depends on the individual soul. The Church calculated time in Purgatory as a sentence measured out in years and even days. You served your time and then were freed. Dante also avails himself of this concept on occasion. The poet Statius, for instance, tells us in *Purgatorio* 22 that he spent centuries "working" on sloth before tackling his sin of prodigality for centuries more. Yet the overall spirit of the *Purgatorio* is far less mechanical. We understand that the proud stand free of their burdensome egos not so much in answer to an external clock as in response to their own maturation. They will ''terminate,'' to recall the analogy of psychoanalysis, when their spiritual work, their conversion of virtue into vice, is complete. When that happy time comes, the mountain shakes with joy as the other penitents sing out, ''Gloria in excelsis Deo,'' as they do for Statius (*Purg.* 20.124–38).

One of Dante's many innovations in the second canticle is his demonstration that art and artists play a significant role in the transformative process of salvation. The point should not be lost on us, for if this is true of art in the purgatorial afterlife, might it not also be true of the world of the living? Featured first and foremost among the *Purgatorio*'s artists, of course, is God, the master craftsman of Heaven and earth, who is ultimately responsible for the pictures we see and the dramas we watch. In the ''waiting room'' at the base of the mountain, just below the Gate of Purgatory, those preparing to begin their ascent are given a pageant of their redemption every evening, as if to prepare them for the dreams of night (8.19–39). More follows in the Garden of Eden, which is located above the seven terraces and at the crest of the mountain. There Dante watches an allegorical procession of biblical revelation in canto 29, and, in canto 32, a presentation of St Paul's theology of the old and new Adam followed by a phantasmagoric reprise of the beleaguered history of the Church.

At both the beginning and end of *Purgatorio,* therefore, God offers artistic representations that reform and renew the minds of the penitents, just as human artistry (including the *Purgatorio* itself) might be said to do. In addition, there are other kinds of art along the way: narrative pictures that seem to come to life, visions or soundscapes that appear and disappear on the terraces, each with its corresponding virtue and vice, each offering the opportunity to learn.

In canto 10, for example, the penitents on the Terrace of Pride are humbled by looking at murals incised upon the mountain's side – works of astonishing realism that appear "more real" than nature itself. Revealing God to be a sculptor without equal, they also suggest that true humility has nothing to do with self-abasement. For what the penitents see are pictures of spiritual heroism: the Virgin Mary's bravery when she dared to say "Yes" to the angel's annunciation; the joyous self-forgetfulness of a naked King David dancing before the Ark of the Lord; and the Emperor Trajan's generosity when, on his way to war, he agreed to do justice for an insignificant widow. Conversely, when the penitents look down upon the pavement of the terrace they see the exemplary images of pride caught in various moments of self-destruction. These hyper-realistic representations, "where the dead seemed dead, and the alive, alive" (*Purg.* 12.67), are meant to be trampled down and left behind. "Reading" these images, even as we read Dante's words, leads to that spiritual renewal which St Paul enjoins in Romans 12:2: "Be not conformed to this world, but be transformed by the renewing of your minds." This text could well serve as an epigraph for the *Purgatorio*.

After art assists the souls in their transformation, ritual takes over to complete the process. Purgatory is as much a prolonged liturgy as it is a "multiplex" of theater, art gallery, and concert. Newly chastened, unencumbered by false notions of importance, the souls are brushed by an angel's wing, discover the erasure of Pride's mark from their foreheads, and hear the appropriate Beatitude from Christ's Sermon on the Mount, "Blessed are the poor in spirit for they shall see God": " '*Beati pauperes spiritu*' was sung / so sweetly – it cannot be told in words" (*Purg.* 12.110–11). The Beatitudes are sung on each terrace, as are other prayers, hymns, and psalms. Rites once neglected on earth are now understood to be sustenance and delight. Hence, the rapturous chanting of the "Te lucis ante," the "Salve regina," and the psalms.

Despite occasional outbursts of sympathy for the pain that Dante either witnesses or anticipates experiencing for himself in the future, it is not the penitents' suffering that the poem dwells on; it is the degree to which art, music, language – beauty of all kinds – assist in personal transformation. The end result of the purgatorial process is joy, freedom, being "crowned and mitered" over oneself (27.142). Thus, while pain is exacted on all the terraces, beauty transforms the soul, with happiness completing the metamorphosis. Not surprisingly, artists (but especially poets) are well represented in the canticle. Either they are present in person – Casella, Sordello, Oderisi da Gubbio, Bonagiunta da Lucca, Guido Guinizelli, Arnaut Daniel, along with Statius – or are spoken about: Franco Bolognese, Cimabue, Giotto. Nor is it possible to overlook the impact that Virgil had on the conversion of Statius as described in canto 22. In the first instance, Statius's reading of an episode in *Aeneid* 3 turned him away from prodigality; in the second, a "consonance" between the enigmatic *Eclogue* 4 and the apostle's teaching led him to embrace the gospel. If pagan poetry can be the agent of a renewed moral life, not to mention of salvation, how much more so the *Commedia*?

In this celebration of artists and poets, be they God the master craftsman or the poets Dante was himself touched by, he is in essence making a case for his own vocation. He shows that the artist's genius can be a gift from God; it can even be a way for a person to reveal his or her identity as made in the image of God. By this account, poetry is an agent of the "new life"; it is not the bridesmaid of theology, but the bride herself.

Reunion with Beatrice

Something like a wedding takes place at the mountain's summit when Dante is reunited with Beatrice (who in the time scheme of the poem died 10 years earlier, in 1290). From the first canto of *Inferno* it was promised she would find him again; the pilgrim also knows she sought out Virgil in Limbo to enlist his aid in rescuing the one lost in the dark wood. From time to time, her name has been lovingly invoked; her beautiful "shining eyes" and gentle speech conjured as an enticement. When finally she does appear in the extraordinarily formal setting of the Pageant of Revelation, rather than rushing into her lover's arms – even if the laws of the afterlife permitted such an act – she scolds and denounces him, making whatever pain he encountered in Purgatory seem preferable to this onslaught. Given the love that had been given to him through her, how could he have abandoned "the way, the truth, and the life" that she opened up?

Apparently, for all the penance that Dante had mimed along the Terraces of the Mountain, it remained for this encounter in Eden to bring his whole life story to a head. The gifts received at birth, the grace bestowed through his meeting with Beatrice, dreams and visions from the time of her death until now – what did it amount to given the spiritual morass represented by his stumbling in the dark wood? By this point in the poem it is clear that Beatrice represents far more than her individual self. Whatever the romance these two Florentine adolescents may have experienced, we are meant to consider their love in its ultimate consequence. From the very beginning, Beatrice was Dante's road to God. How, then, could he have failed to continue upon it? Why did he lose the "true way" (*Inf.* 1.3)?

There is no grand betrayal or apostasy to confess. Dante proffers only a banal truth that anyone might say at the Last Judgment: "Mere appearances / turned me aside with their false loveliness, / as soon as I had lost your countenance" (*Purg.* 31.34–6). In other words, "stuff" got in the way and appearance proved more appealing than reality. In the experience of romantic love, he was shown how to ascend to the "sun and the others stars." But once the beloved was gone – and with her, the incentive to persevere – he fell into the superficial brightness of "present things."

This truth admitted without equivocation, Beatrice relents. Slowly she lifts her veil, first to reveal her eyes and then her mouth. By looking at her open face, Dante is able to catch a foretaste of the radiance that will dazzle him throughout the *Paradiso* – "O splendor of eternal living light" (*Purg.* 31.139). According to the whole trajectory of the *Commedia*, this should be the *telos* or purpose of our fullest loves. We are meant to direct one another to God.

In preparation for paradisiacal ascent, Dante must leave the burdens of the past behind by drinking from the River Lethe. That done, he will take yet another draught, this time of Eunoe, whose waters bring back the memory of good overlooked and graces unacknowledged. This accomplished, there is a new identity for him to assume, as we see when Beatrice twice commands him to look, remember, and, at some later time, write: "Take note; and even as I speak these words, / do you transmit them in your return to those / who live the life that is a race toward death" (*Purg.* 33.52–4). The errant lover and befuddled pilgrim is called to become a prophet, not unlike Isaiah, Ezekiel, or Jeremiah in the Hebrew Bible or John the Divine in the Book of Revelation. Beatrice shows him a vision of history in which Church and State, the See of Peter and the seat of empire, appear in a grotesque metamorphosis of chariot, giant, and whore. At the close of *Purgatorio* Dante glimpses an apocalypse: he is to set it down, as best he can, for his own time and place.

And what of Virgil? In perhaps the most stunning scene in the entire poem (*Purg.* 30.1–54), Virgil disappears from the narrative through a gradual effacement of his own poetry. First appears the solidity of a Latin quote (l. 21), next a vernacular translation of a line from the *Aeneid* (l. 48), and finally an echo of the fourth *Georgic* (ll. 49–51). Distraught, the pilgrim calls out "Virgilio...Virgilio...Virgilio." He acts as would any bereft person desperate to hang on to a lost beloved through the invocation of a name. By this time, the reader also has a great deal to lose. After Virgil slips away between the lines of *Purgatorio* 30, it is as one we have known as friend as well as guide – the *Commedia*'s most appealing character.

Once Beatrice appears on the scene, restored to Dante by the power of the Resurrection, it is time for the pagan Virgil to return to the infernal underworld from whence he came. The *Commedia* is never the same without his presence, nor is Dante ever able to let him go. Recollections of his *Aeneid* continue into the one hundredth canto, with mention there of the Sibyl's light leaves being lost "beneath the wind" (*Par.* 33.65) – the poem's final Virgilian allusion. In this way poetry, like love, turns out to be as strong as death.

Paradiso

The final leg of the journey is the most difficult (see Figure 6). This is not true for Dante the pilgrim, who no longer needs to scramble into hellish ditches or climb up a rigorously demanding mountain; who is no longer pursued by vengeful demons or confronted by a former lover in the mode of hanging judge. In the third canticle, however, our attention shifts from the struggle of the pilgrim to that of the poet, the storyteller who brings him to us and who must now follow through on his promise to "retell the good" (*Inf.* 1.8) that he found at journey's end.

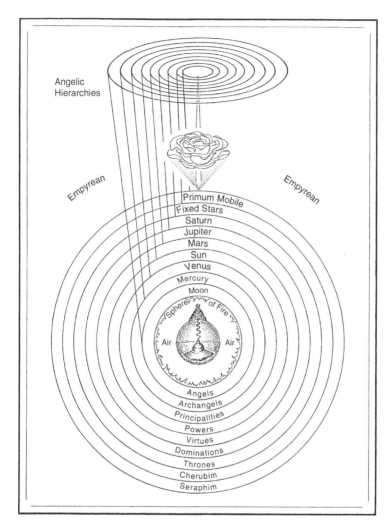

Labels within the figure:

Angelic
Hierarchies

Empyrean

Empyrean

Primum Mobile
Fixed Stars
Saturn
Jupiter
Mars
Sun
Venus
Mercury
Moon
Sphere of Fire
Air
Air

Angels
Archangels
Principalities
Powers
Virtues
Dominations
Thrones
Cherubim
Seraphim

Figure 6 "Dante's Universe"
Courtesy of Robert Henry Turner

This Dante is fully aware of the subject matter he is up against – the vision of God and of realities that cannot be spoken about easily or perhaps at all. He tells us precisely this at the outset. No one has ever chartered these linguistic seas before or spoken the "ineffable words" that St Paul refused to disclose after his own rapture to Heaven (2 Cor. 12:1–2). Dante admits that the-passing-beyond-humanity – an act for which the poet must invent a word, *trasumanar(e)* (*Par.* 1.70) – cannot be put into language. And yet the residue that the poet can remember, the little that he can verbalize, he will set down.

His "official" reason for writing (*Par.* 1.34–6) is hope that the poem's "little spark" will ignite a greater fire, that "better voices" may follow and better prayers (and poems?) be offered after him. Maybe so. Perhaps the powerful ego that was able until now to sustain his work's magnificent effort realizes at this point how little even his genius has to offer. Nonetheless, in the final canticle of the *Commedia* it is impossible not to sense a new upswing in Dante's soaring ambition or imagine anyone else in all of literature who could possibly "do" the ineffable better. For all his avowals of incompetence and failure, which almost become a refrain in the final canto, there is no gainsaying his achievement in the *Paradiso*, either as poet or theologian.

It is not the storyteller alone, however, who must labor over his impossible project; there is also his audience. At the opening of canto 2 Dante tells us that the text will be heavy going, and in a lengthy address to the reader invites those who thus far have only been along for the ride to think seriously about turning back. For good reason! No one can find the *Paradiso* easy sailing once Beatrice starts holding forth on the nature of the cosmos (canto 1), the true reason for the moon's spots (2), the wherewithal for making good on broken vows (5), and God's "rationale" for choosing the Incarnation as a way to redress Adam's primal sin (7). Nor is the voluble Beatrice alone at the podium. Come canto 6, the seventh-century Byzantine

Emperor Justinian (imperial architect of Ravenna) weighs in with 142 uninterrupted lines on the ancient glories and contemporary woes of Empire.

Most readers of the third canticle miss the excitement of Hell, and the sense of becoming new found in Purgatory – in other words, miss the poignant encounters with lost souls or those who are works-in-progress like ourselves. On the contrary, nothing very "personal" happens in the text until Dante's great-great-grandfather appears in the Heaven of Mars and opens up his descendant's future exile (cantos 15– 18). For the first third of the *Paradiso* we get theologically fraught questions meticulously answered in the manner of the Scholastic masters, which only leads to a new crop of questions springing up. The "fit audience, though few" that stays on board will determine whether these prologue cantos constitute high seas or dead calm. Readers formerly educated through a catechism may even experience unpleasant flashbacks. Indeed, it may seem that returning to shore, or simply returning the book to its shelf, is the best option.

This would be a mistake. True, the beginning of the *Paradiso* dares you to enjoy its rite of passage. But no matter how difficult the start-up, the reader, like the pilgrim in the text, should realize that here we are regaining the "good of the intellect" lost in Hell, retrieved in Purgatory, and now ready for a rigorous work-out – or what's a Heaven for? The pilgrim is meant to ask questions, and also to see that answers generate more inquiry. It is *good* to know, to exercise the intellect; it should be a joy to do so. Furthermore, there are *Paradiso* ground rules that need to be established before much time passes.

Learning about glory

First, Beatrice must teach that the apparent diversity of reality has a single source in God, whose divine light is filtered throughout the material universe. What appears to be the Many is in fact the One. In canto 2, a question about the spots on the moon follows this initial exposition. The pilgrim believes (as did Dante himself in the *Convivio*) that the mystery of the markings on the lunar surface – the "man in the moon" – has a material cause. Not so, says Beatrice: the true explanation is entirely spiritual. Once God's spiritual presence penetrates the Primum Mobile and is transmitted as light to the physical spheres, it is received and then passed on by one Heaven, one governing angelic order, after another. Below receives from above, with each "reception" making a distinctive "alloy" that bears more or less of the original undifferentiated light source. Thus, the alloy of the moon is least able to reflect the light and the Primum Mobile the most luminous. Together, the spheres (and the angels that move them) constitute a heavenly choreography, an orchestration that celebrates the One and the Many, a light show celebrating God's Unity and the diversity in which it is apprehended and reflected.

Is the reader still on board? By this point we are only at the end of canto 2! What follows in the sphere of the moon moves us from the cosmic to the personal. Take the powerful Florentine Donati family that Dante knew well once he became Gemma Donati's husband. The pilgrim encounters the soul of Piccarda Donati in the moon, meets her sibling Forese among the penitent Gluttons and hears about her still living brother, Corso, while in Hell. He is disturbed by Piccarda's presence in the heaven that spins slowest and at the greatest remove from the Empyrean. Understanding his dismay, she smiles, as do so many of the blessed, and explains that she is perfectly content with the spiritual station that her momentary appearance in the moon betokens. It is the will of God, "and in his will is our peace" (*Par.* 3.85).

Dante understands these words perfectly well: "every place / in Heaven is in Paradise," he says, "though grace / does not rain equally from the High Good'' (3.88–90). But this does not mean that he likes what he hears any more than do most contemporary readers of the poem. Beatrice honors his problem over the "unfairness" of hierarchy in the following canto, when she assures him that in Paradise God "rains" so abundantly upon each of the blessed that they are all full to overflowing. Every one of the blessed is in the Empyrean: they only *appear* to him in the spheres to signify their spiritual "size place." Each cup is full to overflowing. The fact that some cups are larger than others – that the demitasse, although filled to the brim, holds less than the tankard – means only that different capacities of spirit, as opposed to an identical capacity for beatitude, is part of the divine plan. The "volume" of each human vessel is the product first of God's gift to the individual and then of his or her realization of it. In Heaven, each soul is at capacity.

This variety of gifts and realizations offers another way to understand the cosmic model Beatrice sets forth in *Paradiso* 1. Only now, the "alloy" or "partnership" in question has to do with persons, not planets. Again we see the importance of "the one and the other" and "more and less." There is a single divine Will, and a myriad number of personal actualizations that make up the City of God.

Dante's notion of hierarchy is among the most alien and indeed off-putting features of the *Commedia*. In our world, as Garrison Keillor jokes of his fictional Lake Wobegon, "all the children are above average"; in the same spirit, a certain Boston school advertises itself as a place where "all our students are leaders." Dante would not only think this a lie but a nightmare. For him, "difference" was hard-wired into the nature of things. We are reminded of this frequently, and not only by Beatrice. Justinian observes "differing voices join to sound sweet music; / so do the different orders in our life / render sweet harmony among these spheres" (6.124–6). The Dominican Thomas and the Franciscan Bonaventure each celebrates the founder of the rival order, acknowledging that the Church has been well served by the strikingly different gifts of "the one and the other."

The sticking point here for contemporary readers is probably not the notion of "the one and the other," or of a variety of gifts that are all necessary for a community to flourish (such as St Paul speaks of as the Body of Christ); the difficulty lies with God's involvement in the phenomenon of "more or less." It is not enough that Beatrice reassures that there is not a single bad seat in the Empyrean, or that everyone thrills to the music of the spheres. What rankles is that some who listen take in more, have a deeper connection to the music, and "get it" at a more profound level. This is not just because they practiced more diligently during their lifetime (which is not difficult to accept); it is finally because God gave them their extraordinary gift out of an inscrutable desire to do so.

This inequity does not sit well, especially if it is taken to mean that there is a static order of things determined by birth, that what "is" is meant to be taken as God's will. Such a stasis is definitely not part of Dante's vision: he argues that Fortune, God's angel, rightly keeps her wheel turning so that no one has power or blessing for very long. He is also adamant that virtue, nobility, and the "gentle heart" are *not* inherited through a bloodline. What is most at stake for him is the notion of a providential order at the heart of things, which expresses itself in diversity rather than uniformity. He sees the variability of gifts ultimately as God's business, not our own. What I cannot know or see so fully, you can – a fact that in *Paradiso* (see Chapter 4) produces a grin, not a frown.

Partnership in Paradise

Partnership is a theme as central in *Paradiso* as love in *Purgatorio*. We saw the inability to share writ large in Hell; then we tracked growth in mutuality along the Terraces of the Mountain. Dante learns in *Purgatorio* 15, for instance, that sharing means having more, not less. This is not the case, of course, with material goods: there, less is always less. But with love and light everything changes: "the more there are who say 'ours,' / so much the greater is the good possessed by each – so much more love burned in this cloister" (*Purg.* 15.55–7).

In the third canticle, partnership is also revealed to be the nature of God, whose unity is comprised of the mutual loving of three divine Persons. Central Trinitarian doctrine is celebrated in the Heaven of the Sun, where the great teachers of the Church sing "three times by each and all" the praises of "That One and Two and Three who ever lives / and ever reigns in Three and Two and One, / not circumscribed and circumscribing all" (*Par.* 14.28–30). By the end of the *Commedia*, this mystical mathematics becomes a celebration of God's triune Self:

> You dwell within
> Yourself, and only You know You; Self-knowing,
> Self-known, You love and smile upon Yourself!
> (*Par.* 33.124–7)

Because partnership is God's own truth, is who God *is*, it comes as no surprise to see it expressed among the blessed. When the pilgrim approaches the sphere of Mercury, for instance, each of the souls declares, "Here now is one who will increase our loves" (*Par.* 5.105). In Jupiter, the individual blessed appear in the collective form of an Eagle, who "did utter with its voice both *I* and *mine* / when *we* and *ours* were what, in thought, were meant" (19.11–12). Because they are all centered in God, like spokes in a wheel, the blessed can also see into one another fully: they are of one mind and heart.

The discrepancy between their omniscience and Dante's blinkered understanding causes the pilgrim some frustration in the Heaven of Venus. He complains to Charles Martel – who surely knows his question even before he poses it – "I would not have to wait for your request / if I could enter you as you do me" (9.80–81). This English translation of "s'io m'intuassi, come tu t'inmii" is adequate enough, but the line deserves a more literal rendering. For what the pilgrim does is employ an odd and made up language in order to dramatize the immediacy (not to mention the intimacy) of communication among the blessed. Dante says to Charles Martel, "if I in-you-ed myself, as you in-me-yourself." This same sense of radical intersubjectivity is found throughout the canticle whenever the poet invents reflexive verbs out of nouns and pronouns. One can in-pearl oneself, find oneself in-sapphire, in-future, in-eternity, in-her, in-him, in-Heaven, and in-God.

Language is part of *Paradiso*'s theological adventure – an aspect of the poem's navigation of uncharted seas. Dante would have us believe that he is always at a loss, and thus time and again will pronounce his failure to "transhumanate" (to recall the neologism, *trasumanar(e)*, in *Par.* 1.70). Are these protestations signs of bad faith on the poet's part? Surely he must have realized he succeeded at writing on water, in capturing the ephemeral shimmer of light before it darkens or changes into another kind of shine. But perhaps because Dante knew what he could *not* say, his protestations are not coy but, rather, honest admissions. After all, can anyone "succeed" when describing love, light, or God?

A sense of failure and loss may even be necessary when approaching the Godhead. And so, in the *Paradiso* an image will last as long as a bubble before bursting into airy nothing. A lengthy description will collapse just after being very exactly constructed, when the poet in effect tells us, "That's not what I meant, that's not what I meant at all." Perhaps all a writer burdened by such a project can do is hope that at least a trace of the experience will be left behind, the trajectory of a mis-fired metaphor – *something* understood.

The end of the journey

In the poem's final cantos, and contrary to all expectation, Beatrice is replaced as guide by Bernard of Clairvaux (d. 1153), the contemplative, church reformer, and ardent devotee of the Virgin Mary. None of the sorrow that marked the disappearance of Virgil in *Purgatorio* 30 occurs in *Paradiso* 31. This is because Beatrice has not truly left the pilgrim but only resumed her place in the heavenly rose. When Dante thanks her for what she has done and meant for him, she turns away to resume her gaze upon that "eternal fountain" who is God. No tears are shed, no triple stutter of her name such as we heard in Eden with "Virgilio . . . Virgilio . . . Virgilio."

By the beginning of the *Commedia*'s 100th canto, the circle that opened up in *Inferno* 1 draws to its close. Bernard entrusts the pilgrim to the Virgin Mary, whose intervention on his behalf first sent Beatrice to Limbo and Virgil to the "dark wood." Bernard's intercessory prayer fills the Virgin with de-light, and so she, like Beatrice before her, turns her face upward to the divine light. Dante does not need to be told to do likewise. He effortlessly follows the drift, borne aloft on a tide no sailor in his right mind would want to resist.

From this point on, the poet alternates between avowals of what he cannot say and fragments of what he saw. First, the whole of the universe like a million scattered pages seems brought together and bound by love into one volume. Then, that "book" becomes three circles of the same dimension but of distinct coloration. Finally, within the central circle, he sees come into focus "la nostra effige" (33.131), "our image" – the face of the One who looks like us but who, in fact, made us in his divine image.

Even at this 11th hour of the journey, the knottiest doctrinal questions come flooding. How can God be three and one, or Christ be "light from light, true God of true God" and at the same time the Word-made-flesh? Weighed down by the central dogmas of Trinity and Incarnation, the poet recalls himself with a sense of humor. The man once lost in a dark wood struggles to rationalize mysteries that cannot be disentangled even by genius. A geometer comes to mind, hopelessly intent on squaring the circle. The task cannot be done! But then it does not have to be. Experience overwhelms the rational mind, and the pilgrim finds himself transported into the reality of God by the love that moves the sun and the other stars. As the poet then falls into silence, we arrive at the resonant "failure" of the *Commedia*'s magnificent close.

Chapter 3

Dante's Beatrice

There comes a time in every Dante class when someone blows the whistle on Beatrice.[1] Until then, she's safe. The obsession with Eros and romantic love present everywhere in popular music and cinema – an opiate of the people if ever there was one – has kept the students sympathetic to her. Dante falling in love and then suffering the consequences make immediate sense; so too does the draw of physical beauty and (at least in principle) the pledge of faithfulness to a beloved. Despite a revolving door of relationships and "hook-ups," the words of a 1950s crooner articulate their conviction if not their reality: "When I fall in love it will be forever." As a result, Dante's pursuit of Beatrice in the *Vita Nuova*, her rescue of him through the intervention of Virgil at the outset of the *Commedia*, and the way she functions as a lure to get him through the thick and thin of Hell and Purgatory all meet with approval. Her love keeps lifting him higher.

Then the moment of truth. It usually takes place when the students come to a scene at the Edenic summit of Purgatory mentioned in Chapter 2 but worth reconstructing here: it is possibly the most intricately wrought encounter in the entire poem. Directly across the River Lethe from a transfixed Dante comes a procession of venerable men who collectively present the Christian Bible, both Old and New Testaments. At the center of the grouping is a griffin (part eagle, part lion) that draws what appears at first to be an empty chariot. Immediately surrounding it are the four "living creatures" taken from Ezekiel and Revelation that traditionally represent the Gospels; flanking them are dancing maidens who personify the seven virtues. For most students the scene opens up alien territory, accessible if at all only for those whose memory goes back to the recent televised funerals of a princess or a pope – astonishing, intricate solemnities full of symbolic weight as well as emotional power.

The Advent of Beatrice

At the beginning of *Purgatorio* 30, voices sing significant Latin texts as clouds of flowers are hurled into the radiant air by angelic hands. Standing on the left side of the chariot (it wasn't empty after all) appears the very lady we have been waiting for since the opening of the poem. She wears a crimson dress, just as she did as a nearly nine-year-old girl when Dante saw her for the first time, as recalled in the *Vita Nuova*. She is also veiled in white and therefore shielded from the hunger and thirst of the pilgrim's gaze. Nonetheless, he recognizes her unmistakable "hidden force." He is shaken, stupefied, all but consumed by an erotic fire that dissolves the barrier of the intervening years separating this reunion from the time when he first fell in love. "I felt the mighty power of old love" (30.39), he acknowledges, quoting the exact title of one of his earlier love lyrics. He then confides to Virgil, "I recognize the signs of the ancient flame" (l. 48), using a line that comes from the fourth book of Virgil's own *Aeneid*. Then, turning to share the wonder of this lady with his beloved master, Dante suddenly realizes that he is no longer there:

> [For] Virgil had deprived us of himself,
> Virgil, the gentlest father, Virgil, he
> to whom I gave myself for my salvation.
> (*Purg.* 30.49–52)

The Problem of Beatrice

Sooner or later this simultaneous departure and arrival had to happen: Virgil told the pilgrim to expect it from the very first canto of the poem. But not like this! For rather than meeting the angelic lady of the *Vita Nuova*, or the weeping, solicitous intercessor we heard about in *Inferno* 2, there is someone altogether unexpected inside that crimson dress and snow-white veil:

> "Dante, though Virgil's leaving you, do not
> yet weep, do not weep yet; you'll need your tears
> for what another sword must yet inflict."
> (*Purg.* 30.55–7)

The lady is not joking. In the lines that follow, and through most of the next canto, she roars at the bereft pilgrim like a drill sergeant on a rant or like an exasperated mother at the end of a long day. "Look here! For I am Beatrice! I am!" (l. 73) is her war cry.

Students are always taken aback – and angry. The now departed Virgil was a selfless rescuer, tireless guide, gentlest of fathers and, contrary to all patriarchal expectations of a Roman *pater*, "mommy" and "wet nurse" too (*Purg.* 21.97–8). They love him. By contrast, they find Beatrice an ice queen. There are no words of welcome or affection from her. Nor will she abide any weeping, at least not for Virgil. She declines to play along with the romantic expectations that the *Commedia* has itself raised from the first mention of "her gleaming, tearful eyes" (*Inf.* 2.116) to the perceived heat of her veiled presence standing in Eden. She may be his "antica fiamma" (*Purg.* 30.48), but the ancient flame is a very icy fire. Taking no prisoners, Beatrice's tongue is a two-edged sword, and her ferocity astonishing even to her female companions, who might well be expected automatically to play "back up" to her harangue and have no mind of their own. Rather, witnessing her excess, even they plead for moderation: "Lady, why shame him so?" (*Purg.* 30.96).

"Good question!" opines one of the students. Then the class goes wild. The hockey player who has yet to say a word cries out, "What a bitch!" The ardent feminist, taking umbrage at his language, weighs in, "This poem is so not good for women!" And then the class Lothario, who has just caught on, asks with furrowed brow, "You mean to say that this lady that Dante still has a thing for is, like, *dead*? That's sick!" One might dismiss these intemperate, vernacular objections as yet another sign that education is wasted on the young and the barbarians no longer just outside the gates. But the students raise questions that are, in fact, worth pondering. Not to do so is to relinquish the *Commedia*'s relevance to the Middle Ages and thereby, for most readers, to put it back on the shelf.

For surely, the objectors have a point. After all, does Beatrice's high dudgeon prove only that hell hath no fury like a dead woman scorned? Should the deceased, even one clothed in the light of the Resurrection, have so much power over the living? A vow of celibacy to one's deceased beloved has never been enjoined on believers, nor was Queen Victoria's indefatigable mourning for her lost Albert necessarily the faithful way to deal with a beloved's death. No Christian widower can lawfully throw himself on the funeral pyre of his wife, so why should Dante in effect be expected to so do when the healthy thing, after all, is to "move on"? Students become particularly indignant on this point. What right did Beatrice have to take Dante so furiously to account for his alleged waywardness when they were never married in the first place, when they never even had sex?

Beatrice is a tough sell for the contemporary reader, and indeed she may always have been so. The early commentators turned her into Theology (just as they reduced Virgil to Reason) and thereby evaded the problems of her representation: "she" was a way of speaking about other things. Boccaccio held another position. On the basis of conversations with Dante's nephew and a second cousin of one Bice Portinari, he insisted that she was based on flesh and blood, was a childhood neighbor of Dante who shared a Florentine circle with him and had an historical identity (and, it turns out, a prosperous banker husband).

Maybe so. Certainly both the *Vita Nuova* and the *Commedia* lose force (and a great deal of interest) if Beatrice is taken to be only an idea and not a mortal human being. The poet suggests no other identity. Nonetheless, it must be said that when she is introduced in his "libello," she is a vision, pearl of great price rather than a person. She essentially says nothing and has nothing particular about her. Nor does it make sense to call this Florentine pair "lovers" if by that term one means participators in a reciprocal affair. For although Dante and Beatrice run into one another, either according to the dictates of providence or the good offices of the god of Love, they do not meet by mutual agreement. They also never touch, let alone "have sex." The most we can say is that the Beatrice of the *Vita Nuova* notices Dante and is occasionally put off by his antics. She reserves her emotions for her father's death and perhaps for the female friends who surround her. Otherwise she is opaque.

Despite Boccaccio's avowals of her humanity, and what I believe to be Dante's insistence on her historicity as a given, it is difficult not to see at least the *Vita Nuova*'s Beatrice as a literary construct with a long lineage. Her ''bloodline'' dates back to the French romances, the Provençal troubadours, the courtier sonneteers of Sicily, the lyrics and canzone of the early thirteenth-century Bolognese Guido Guinizelli, and to the young intellectual Florentine poets among whom Dante counted himself. It was for them he brought together his scattered lyrics of the 1280s and 1290s and forged them into a coherent narrative ''anatomy'' of his love life with Beatrice. Looking back upon this literary line-up, none of the ladies is individually memorable, no matter how each poet protests that his beloved's beauty and virtue are unique. Convention rules: one ''unique'' size basically fits all.

The Novelty of Beatrice

And yet there is indeed something new about Beatrice and therefore about the *Vita Nuova*. The troubadour poets typically fell in love with idealized women who made them better persons. Guido Guinizelli later likened his beloved to an angel, but did so in a playful spirit that let the reader know he was using hyperbole. The ''sweet new style'' cultivated by Dante's circle went on to raise the ante. The lady was an angel, one of the heavenly intelligences who through their knowledge and love of God make the planets go round; she was a star and her influence as real and effective as any constellation.[2]

Dante raises the stake even higher, however, in the Christological associations he brings to bear on Beatrice in the *Vita Nuova*. One day, Dante sees Beatrice walking behind Cavalcanti's beloved, Vanna; he likens the latter to John the Baptist, the forerunner of "the true light," and Beatrice to Christ. When he has a premonition of her death, the sun grows dark, disoriented birds fall from the sky, the earth shakes – precisely what happened when Christ gave up the ghost. About her own "Passion" and death he cannot speak directly, but nonetheless frames the event with a quote from the Lamentations of Jeremiah (1:1) traditionally associated with Holy Week. The final poem of the *Vita Nuova* imagines Beatrice ascended into Heaven. In the closing paragraph, after mentioning a "wonderful vision" he is not yet ready to describe, Dante prays that one day he may behold Beatrice in Heaven, "who in glory gazes upon the face of Him *qui est per omnia secula benedictus* [who is for all ages blessed]." A vernacular love story culminates in liturgical Latin and the lady's beatific vision of God.

Dante not only maintains but intensifies Beatrice's Christological associations when he reintroduces her in the *Commedia*. She takes on other lofty identities as well: *Sapientia* or Wisdom, Boethius's Lady Philosophy, the Blessed Virgin Mary – the greatest female bringer of beatitude – whose cult as a beautiful maiden (rather than a matronly Mother of God) flourished at the same time as the idealized women of the secular poets traced above. Unlike these ladies, however, this new Beatrice is no silent partner, nor do beauty and virtue sum up her mystery. She speaks at length and with enormous authority. Like all the blessed, her mind is centered in God; she knows the truth and the truth sets her free – free to function in the court of Heaven as does no one else, male or female. She is a theologian-preacher, who rockets beyond Aquinas and Bonaventure when they appear in the Heaven of the Sun; who sits across from St Augustine in the City of God. She plays a role in the afterlife that no mortal woman could ever hope to enjoy in fourteenth-century Florence or, for that matter, in the Vatican of today. Dante's beloved does infinitely more than grace the *Paradiso* with her silent beauty; she presides over it.

Most daringly, however, Beatrice functions throughout the *Commedia* as a figure of Christ. Like the Savior, she descends into Hell in order to rescue ("harrow") the lost – in her case, to bring about Dante's salvation from an infernal dark wood. At her first appearance in Purgatory she is greeted by the acclamation that Christ received on the palm-strewn streets of Jerusalem, "*Benedictus qui venis*" (*Purg.* 30.19), "Blessed are you who come." Grammar would demand that the lady be "benedicta," but the poet retains the masculine ending of "benedictus" in Latin in order to reinforce the connection between his Lord and this lady. When Beatrice later looks at the griffin in *Purgatorio* 31, Dante sees reflected in her eyes first one nature of the "two-natured" beast and then the other. Thus she introduces him to what theologians call the "hypostatic union" of human and divine in Christ. By contemplating his own personal mediator between God and humankind, in other words, he is given insight into the mystery of Christ.

Bidding Adieu

After the actual close of the *Paradiso* – in some hypothetical 101st canto – Dante and Beatrice might be imagined as beholding God "face to face" together, along with the whole company of Heaven. This is where their romance has taken them. By projecting us into a 101st canto, of course, I am going where no critic is meant to go – off the final page and beyond what the poet decided (or was able) to give us. Nonetheless, something like the scenario I am fabricating is suggested by

Dante's final words to Beatrice in the poem. In *Paradiso* 31, expecting to find her standing next to him as she had been throughout his ascent, he discovers that she has been replaced by a kindly old man – the twelfth-century St Bernard of Clairvaux! Amazed, and no doubt disappointed at this replacement, he asks, "Where is she?" (l. 63). Bernard responds at first by assuring Dante that he has come in Beatrice's stead in order to "terminate" his desire –"A terminar lo tuo disiro" (l. 65). It is a reminder that his love properly transcends Beatrice as its object: she is not the "end" at all.

Bernard directs him to look up through the petals of Heaven's white rose and behold the lady's quite specific placement in Paradise, just below the maternal figures of the Virgin Mary and Eve, and next to the Old Testament Rachel, beloved wife of Jacob and mother of Joseph and Benjamin. Such company she keeps! We note the complete absence of abstraction or personification in these ranks. There are only historical persons, and among the myriad unnamed Bernard singles out the ancestors of Christ, some disciples, and less than a handful of saints of the eminence of Francis and Benedict. Among these is Beatrice, the sole contemporary figure present and no doubt a total surprise to a fourteenth-century reader. But there she is, placed alongside a matriarch of Israel – on her own, quite apart from Dante and his drama.

Seeing her as if for the first time, Dante bids his lady a lengthy adieu:

> "O lady, you in whom my hope gains strength,
> you who, for my salvation, have allowed
> your footsteps to be left in Hell, in all
>
> the things that I have seen, I recognize
> the grace and benefit that I, depending
> upon your power and goodness, have received.
>
> You drew me out from slavery to freedom,

by all those paths, by all those means that were
within your power. Do, in me, preserve
   your generosity, so that my soul,
which you have healed, when it is set loose from
my body, may be a soul that you will welcome."
   So did I pray. And she, however far
away she seemed, smiled, and she looked at me.
Then she turned back to the eternal fountain.

                                   (*Par.* 31.79–93)

Inevitably, this leave-taking recalls Virgil's departure from the poem, when Dante turned to discover that his beloved companion was no longer standing next to him, when he was overcome by tears for the one to whom he said he owed his salvation (*Purg.* 30.51). At that time, recognition of his loss came too late for him to thank his master. His tears, therefore, had a specifically Virgilian quality to them, poignant with a sense of missed opportunity and hope cut off.

In this parallel moment in *Paradiso* 31, however, Dante is able to say everything that he wants to say, and to someone who, although no longer positioned next to him, seems close at hand. There is no cause for tears; instead, what we note on Beatrice's face is the flash of a smile – an expression that is (see Chapter 4) one of the poet's trademarks.

So too is his technique of carefully reworking an earlier scene to artfully turn it around. In *Purgatorio* 30 Dante celebrated Virgil as the agent of his liberation: "Virgil, the gentlest father, Virgil, he / to whom I gave myself for my salvation" (ll. 50–1). Here it is Beatrice who is remembered in that capacity – she who came to Virgil in the first circle of the Inferno in order to bring about Dante's rebirth. Therefore he speaks to her as "you who, for my salvation, have allowed your footprints to be left in Hell." Without apology – we are beyond all such notions here – he simply reorients his praise. He could be saved by Virgil only because Beatrice had visited Hell to intercede on her lover's behalf.

Applied Christology seems to have reached new heights in this moment of prayerful reckoning: Beatrice is his savior. And yet the passage also presents us with a new stage in Dante's *personal* relationship with Beatrice. In lieu of the respectful "voi" that he has used with her throughout the *Commedia*, she becomes a different "you" – an intimate, familiar "tu." Perhaps this move from formal to informal, which is also a shift from the plural "voi" to the singular "tu," suggests that, for all the religious aura of his praise, Dante is now addressing the unadorned Beatrice, set free from the symbolic encumbrances she has borne. The lady who smiles and then turns away to the eternal fountain is not the maiden floating through the spectral city of the *Vita Nuova*. Nor is she the magisterial scold of the Edenic reunion, or the bemused grownup who rolls her eyes when Dante fails to "get it" in Paradise as she lectures tirelessly on beatitude. She is not even the caring mother who feeds, comforts, and praises her offspring in *Paradiso* 23. Rather, in the poem's 11th hour we have the human "face to face" moment we have been waiting for. A man talks to a woman he loves.

Dante speaks his piece to Beatrice in what turns out to be his longest address to her in the poem. Although she says nothing in response, it is not because (as in the conventions of love poetry) it would be indecorous for the lady to respond. *Paradiso* gives us abundant proof that she can be relentlessly verbal! But not now. Perhaps she refrains from speaking because she is moved by Dante's gratitude, because what he has said has touched her. If so, then this is another hint of her emotional reciprocity among the few that have been given, the tears she first sheds for Dante when speaking to Virgil in Limbo and the fury she vents over his forgetting after her death.

To my mind at least, Beatrice is never more real as a character than in her reluctance to say anything at all in *Paradiso* 31. Listening to Dante speak the truth, she is at a loss and therefore human at last. For a moment she is not a saint whose mind is "in God" and thus incapable of surprise. On the contrary, she is taken aback. All she can do in response is smile at the man who thanks her. And then she turns away, back to the source of all love, the deep and abiding fountain who is God.

This partnership sealed by a smile may well be what the poet understands holy Eros to be. The goal of love is a face-to-face encounter with the beloved that does not end simply in a human exchange, however rich; rather, it leads both lovers to God. For this reason my fantasy of a 101st canto has both Dante and Beatrice joined together *not* gazing into one another's eyes but looking side by side at something – at Someone – else.

Beatrice has indeed been working toward this end, ironically, ever since she blamed Dante for turning away from her in the past. When he cannot bring himself to look at anything but her unveiled eyes and mouth at the end of *Purgatorio*, he is not rewarded for his new-found obsession. He's told that he has become fixated on his beloved. "Troppo fisso!" (32. 11), "Too fixed!" as Beatrice's companions call out. In *Paradiso*'s Heaven of the Sun, she actually smiles when his attention to her is eclipsed by his gratitude to God (*Par.* 10.55–60). Later on, when he is staring into her eyes and *not* looking elsewhere, she reminds him, "not only in my eyes is paradise . . . " (18.21).

A lady reorienting the fixation of her lover's gaze, turning away from him with a smile on her lips? This marks the complete reversal of the love affair of Paolo and Francesca, presented in *Inferno* 5 and a point of reference throughout the *Commedia*. The poet gives us the infernal couple as storm-tossed lovers locked in an eternal embrace, gazing into one another's eyes in an infinite regression of mutual regard. "You are the world to me," they seem to say to one another. Yet in the context of Hell, the avowal seems like a prison sentence rather than a declaration of true love. Their coupling is the antithesis of the two who look at one another within the heavenly rose before the lady turns to God and, in a canto's time, her lover follows suit.

Eros and Sex in the Commedia

When I speak of Dante and Beatrice as a couple, I must for accuracy's sake make clear than I am not talking about erotic union, neither its beginning in an unattended kiss – Paolo and Francesca's downfall – nor its consummation in sexual intercourse. One must imagine a relationship more "full-blooded" than the shadow play of the *Vita Nuova*, certainly, but without the knowledge of sexual partners or the long history of a couple who have spent time together in bed.

Nonetheless, the Beatrice of the *Commedia* has Eros aplenty, and on both sides of the grave. Not only did her "youthful eyes" and "beautiful limbs" once hold the young Dante captive in Florence; not only did he hunger and thirst for her in such a way that her reduction to an allegory of Theology becomes preposterous; but she is an old flame now burning brighter than ever. Encountered in the afterlife, she is in the prime of a greater beauty, as we are told every time in *Paradiso* when Dante looks into her eyes and finds her still more ravishing. The "second life" becomes her as a woman: she is a saint with a red dress on.

But this erotic charge has to do with divinity, *not* humanity, so that we would do better to speak of a theological Eros than of romantic love. Sexuality concerns the mortal body, not that heavenly body that Christian doctrine affirms will be the joy of the blessed after the General Resurrection at the end of time, but which (ever since St Paul raised the topic in 1 Corinthians

15) it has not been able to define. As Dante knew from Jesus's own words, "For in the resurrection they shall neither marry nor be married; but shall be as the angels of God in heaven" (Matt 22:30). Desire may well be powerful in Paradise, but it leads to the *spiritual* intercourse of the blessed with one another and with God.

Certainly, the poet uses the language of profane love – sparks and flames, the "old net" of passion (*Purg.* 32.6), and even the love bites of ecstasy (*Par.* 26.51) – to describe Beatrice's effect on him. And then there is heavenly charity as it is experienced by the blessed. How else to represent the profound spiritual longing of Heaven but through the sensual appetite that enthralls and drives us on earth? The mystical interpretation of the biblical Song of Songs had long established sensual language as a way to explore the spirit. The Bride of the Song was understood to be not only the individual soul but the Church, the Bridegroom's "body." Thus, in the Paradise that Beatrice opens up in the final canticle, *everyone* is in love, so that the exclusive affection of earthly married couples that the *Commedia* on one occasion celebrates (*Purg.* 25.134–5) becomes in Heaven a corporate and inclusive partnership of all saints. For this reason when Dante ascends to the Heaven of Mercury he is met immediately by "more than a thousand splendors" who together cry out, "Here now is one who will increase our loves" (*Par.* 5.105). The poet likens them to fish rushing to the surface of their pond at the proximity of something to eat. The community of the blessed craves a new arrival *that* much.

Paolo and Francesca, Dante and Beatrice

Many of these issues – the Eros of Heaven, the proper ordering of loves, sensual language for spiritual experience – come together early in the third canticle. On the brink of *Paradiso* 5, a world away from Paolo and Francesca's *Inferno* 5, Dante asks a question: if a sacred vow is broken, is it ever possible to mend the breach by some other act? The inquiry arises naturally in context and does not seem likely to spark a passionate exchange. One imagines, rather, the tedium of the classroom: a conscientious theology student, looking for a textbook case, approaches his revered professor, who will no doubt respond in the fashion of a medieval Scholastic by marshaling the appropriate authorities on vow-breaking and its possible remedies. Instead of a dry academic comeback, however, Beatrice responds to her pupil in ways that nowadays would lead to censure if not to loss of position.

> Beatrice looked at me with eyes so full
> of sparks of love, eyes so divine that my
> own force of sight was overcome, took flight,
> and eyes downcast, I almost lost my senses.
>
> (*Par.* 4.139–42)

With this cliff-hanger bringing *Paradiso* 4 to a close, we then receive Beatrice's considered answer at the very outset of the fifth, "Francescan" canto that follows:

> "If in the flame of love I seem to flame
> beyond the measure visible on earth,
> so that I overcome your vision's force,
>   you need not wonder; I am so because
> of my perfected vision. . . . "
>
> (*Par.* 5.1–5)

Beatrice goes on to say that, in Dante's curiosity about the satisfaction of broken vows, she discerns the glimmer of the "never-ending light" – God's light. Dante's intellect is aroused, and so in turn is hers; he sparks her into a more intense radiance. In Heaven, it is intellect that inspires passion. The keener one sees, the brighter one flames, the hotter one burns.

Beatrice then makes a distinction between greater and lesser loves that takes us to the *mortal* heart of the matter: she speaks to Dante not about the blessed but about those like himself who are still in the flesh. To long for knowledge, according to the heavenly perspective, is to long for nothing less than God. But not every desire or flame on earth is godly.

> and if a lesser thing allure your love,
> it is a vestige of that light which – though
> imperfectly – gleams through that lesser thing.
> *(Par.* 5.10–12)

There are lower loves as well as higher. In the lower, there may be, however imperfect, vestiges of the Real Thing. But it would be a mistake to confuse imperfect with perfect, a good with God.

Inferno 5 provides a perfect example of this confusion when Paolo and Francesca turn Eros into God Almighty. So too does Dante's past abandonment of Beatrice, when a pretty girl or the most recent newcomer in the flesh, "pargoletta, / o altra novità" *(Purg.* 31.59–60), confused his priorities and led him into the dark wood. "Mere appearances/ turned me aside with their false loveliness," he confides through his tears, "as soon as I had lost your countenance" (31.34–6). In other words, once you were dead, I lost interest.

"Human, all too human," one thinks. After a great love that seemingly changed the world, the bereaved forget what has been learned; they lose track even of themselves, that is, of the richer, deeper self that the deceased had nurtured into being. It now seems enough that a new body just be warm. We are meant to deplore this situation: indeed, until Dante confesses it, he cannot see Beatrice face-to-face or be washed in the waters of Eden. But what was actually meant to happen to his own sexuality after Beatrice was no longer in the flesh? Was it simply to be, as the pious were once enjoined, "offered up"? Was sexuality to be denied altogether, so that there is no real place for physical Eros in this scheme of things? If so, then talk about the "flames of love" burning "beyond the measure visible on earth" must be seen as transcending the earth altogether or at least any earthly satisfaction. Then the only erotic passion that the *Commedia* can be said to celebrate is an eroticized spirituality, and preferably focused on a lover who no longer has a body that can (in the biblical sense) be known.

Yet Dante is by no means "against" the body. He has Solomon tell us in the Heaven of the Sun that the blessed long for the General Resurrection when their spirits will be reunited with some semblance of their flesh so that once again they are whole beings. Indeed, when the rest of his company hear Solomon proclaim their expectation of this future moment, the quickness of their "Amen" reveals the ardor of their longing – not only for their own (now dead) bodies but also "perhaps, for / their mothers, fathers, and for others dear / to them before they were eternal flames" (*Par.* 14.64–6). Note the explicit mention of parents, the implicit inclusion of children, but the withheld identity of "others dear / to them." Perhaps lovers or spouses need no mention because they go without saying?

Although there was much speculation about what the resurrected flesh would be like, Dante opts for a continuity of the new body with the old. Beatrice looks as she once did, when (as in the days of the *Vita Nuova*) the sight of her red dress was all the poet needed to forgive, forget, and say, "Love." About the body of Gemma Donati – the woman to whom Dante was betrothed at the age of 12, later married, and with whom he had four children – we know nothing, even though she was wife and mother in the year 1300, the fictional date of the poem, and throughout the years of its composition.

Dante's Sexuality

We have, in fact, no idea how Dante conducted his own sexual life either before or after his solitary exile. In his biography, Boccaccio speaks of the poet's propensity for lechery, which may well have been corroborated by those who "knew him when." Or the poet's lustfulness may only have been deduced from his writing. The one and only purgatorial torment Dante undergoes is on the Terrace of Lust in *Purgatorio* 26, where a great deal is made of his terror over entering the refining fires along with the long file of homosexuals and heterosexuals who dance their way clean of love's imperfections. Dante's presence in the flames may have been an admission that this particular propensity to sin is one he knows to be his own.

Boccaccio's indictment of lechery may also have come from reading the "La Pietra" poems written sometime between the *Vita Nuova* and the *Commedia*. Here Dante exchanges kid gloves for black leather. I am thinking in particular of "Così nel mio parlar voglio esser aspro," "I want to be as harsh in my speech as this fair stone is in her behavior." The stony lady (*La Pietra*) offends by her indifference to the poet's almost homicidal passion, which he in turn blames entirely on her. It's *her* fault that he writhes in an agony of erotic frustration; therefore she must pay. His imagined twirling of her curly blonde hair soon turns nasty. He will *make* her love him, even if rape (lasting as long as the monastic day of tierce, matins, and vesper) is the violent means to that end:

> Once I'd taken in my hand the fair locks which have
> become my whip and lash, seizing them before tierce

I'd pass through vespers with them and the evening bell:
and I'll not show pity or courtesy, O no, I'd be like a bear
at play. And though Love whips me with them now, I would
take revenge more than a thousand fold. Still more, I'd gaze
into those eyes whence come the sparks that inflame my
heart which is dead within me; I'd gaze into them close and
fixedly, to revenge myself on her for fleeing me as she does;
and then with love I would make our peace.

("Così nel mio parlar voglio esser aspro," ll. 66–78,
Foster and Boyde 1967 translation)

This poem reads like the diary of a stalker. It is a fantasy of
entrapment and revenge in which the beloved is battered,
mauled, and tormented until her suitor decides to relent in
his attack once he achieves his release. Then he'll let her go.
"Love" has little to do with it.

There is no reason to assume that this savage poem is an
accurate account of Dante's sexuality any more than to imagine the swooning self-portrait in the *Vita Nuova* describes
what he was really like in his youth. A writer is free to try
things out in words rather than deeds. What we find in this
lyric, however, is evidence that he was perfectly capable of
imagining the dark side of Eros. It makes the trembling kiss of
Paolo and Francesca seem like innocent child's play, and at the
very least shows him a quite credible candidate for much more
than a monastic day spent in the flames of the Terrace of Lust.

If we ask what the poet of the *Commedia* holds out as an ideal
sexual life, we must pay attention to the voices singing from
within the "burning road" of this particular terrace. They offer
the Church's two official options. The first is virginity – Mary
protesting to the Angel of the Annunciation, "How shall this
be done, because I know not man?" (Luke 1:34). To then
provide an instance of resolute maidenhood from the classical
world, the singers go on to recall the goddess Diana, the chaste

huntress, who could not abide among her followers anyone infected with the "poison of Venus" (*Purg.* 25.130–2).

In these first two cases, perpetual virginity is the prescription: no sex is good sex. But abstention is *not* the only path celebrated. The voices within the flames also sing the virtues of the married life: "they praised aloud those wives and husbands who were chaste, / as virtue and as matrimony mandate" (25.133–5). Here Dante is following traditional medieval norms, although giving a little more than usual attention to the sanctity of the married life, as one might expect a married layman to do.

But what is chaste married love? In a theological perspective that went back to St Augustine, the mandate of matrimony was procreation. Husbands and wives properly did their duty to God and Dame Nature. Married virtue kept passion and pleasure as far away as possible from the marriage bed lest the baser senses lead the couple astray from the reproductive raison d'être of their union. If only the husband and wife could sow seed as coolly as the farmer in his field! Heat, even in marriage, was dangerous. According to Aquinas, a man's lust for his own wife was a venial sin, but if he treated her full throttle like an imaginary stranger – with sex for pleasure alone and not for procreation – the *peccatum* or sin was mortal. (A woman's appetites never come up for consideration in these teachings.) Sex was sanctioned by the Edenic command to increase and multiply, but sex without "multiplication" was a grave wrong.

Or it was wrong *unless* Eros was sublimated to charity's still more excellent way – a marriage of true minds in which passion for the other person transcends the urges of the body. This would seem to be the kind of sublimation held up to the reader in Dante's love for Beatrice. The beauty of the beloved leads one to God's beauty; the power of *antico amor* in the flesh is transformed into an *amor nuovo* in the spirit. Sex is not eradicated but transfigured. One might not be a virgin but still love someone chastely; one could even be an ardent spouse in ways that transcended the duties of the conjugal bed by loving without sex.

There is no pairing off in Heaven. At the General Resurrection souls will "as the angels of God in heaven" (Matt. 22:30). Unlike Milton's angels in *Paradise Lost*, Dante's celestial ranks do not enjoy the easy in-and-out imagined by that Protestant exponent of wedded love (and the admissibility of divorce!). "Let it suffice thee that thou know'st / Us happie," the archangel Raphael tells an Adam curious to know if angels enjoy anything like what he has with his unfallen Eve. Yes, Raphael blushes to admit, the angels *do* make love,

> and without Love no happiness.
> Whatever pure thou in the body enjoy'st
> (And pure thou wert created) we enjoy
> In eminence, and obstacle find none
> Of membrane, joynt, or limb, exclusive barrs:
> Easier then Air with Air, if Spirits embrace,
> Total they mix, Union of Pure with Pure
> Desiring; nor restrain'd conveyance need
> As Flesh to mix with Flesh, or Soul with Soul.
> (*Paradise Lost* 8.621–9)

Dante does not go out on this limb, either in imagining angels or their human counterparts in Heaven. Perhaps the closest he comes to suggesting enjoyment "in eminence," the "Union of Pure with Pure," is in his celebration of the relationship between mother and child. We see this when the blessed show their deep affection for Mary. The poet likens them collectively to an infant in the dewy, flushed moment just *after* it has sucked its fill, "when it has taken / its milk, [and] extends its arms out to its mother, / its feeling kindling in an outward flame" (*Par.* 23.121–3). This may be as near as we come in the *Commedia* to realized sensual intimacy, to something like a postcoital *bonheur* – the particular Eros of Mother and Child at the breast. Expressing this enduring bond, the one adoring person-to-person gaze we see within the heavenly rose is that of Anna, Mary's mother. She cannot keep her eyes off her daughter: "Facing Peter / Anna is seated, so content to see her daughter / that, as Anna sings hosannas, she does not move her eyes" (*Par.* 32.133–5).

If this experience of sanctioned sensual pleasure marks a limit to what Dante imagined physical intimacy could be legitimately – if the mutual delight of a nursing mother and her well-fed baby suggest most adequately the beatific fulfillment of a godly life in the flesh – then much of human Eros remains entirely outside the purview of the poem. Overtly, Dante seems to sanction only chaste couples doing their duty but otherwise refraining from sex, or experiencing the kind of sublimation exemplified in the relationship with Beatrice. It is a highly charged, overtly sensual, but ultimately spiritual friendship. The lover must look with wonder on the beloved, acknowledge that beatitude has been revealed in the flesh, but never touch.[3]

The Beatrice explored in this chapter may be a disappointing character. Perhaps Dante was trying to do too many things at once. Beatrice was one of the golden beauties of the courtly love tradition. She functioned like the Redeemer, held forth like a Scholastic theologian, and, at least on one occasion, behaved like a woman happy to finally be receiving her rightful praise. Whereas Virgil is a consistent literary character, as ample as a shade can be, Beatrice largely seems to be a composite of ideas. She comes off as unreal, and to my knowledge has never won a convert for the *Commedia*. Perhaps the lesson here is that a surfeit of meanings can block an experience of the meaningful and the mystery of a person be lost in the shuffle of a puzzle's component parts.

Nonetheless, if Beatrice is unconvincing as a character, even an aesthetic failure, what Dante attempts through her compels attention. Eros has a theology of its own, as he reminds us throughout his work, and the beloved's smile (see Chapter 4) can open up an entire universe.

A Beloved in the Flesh

Some of the poet's twentieth-century readers have found Dante an inspiration for the kind of mutual, adult, embodied love that actually eludes both the *Vita Nuova* and the *Commedia*. In his 1943 study, *The Figure of Beatrice*, Charles Williams put into circulation an intensely personal reading of the poet.[4] Whereas T. S. Eliot (for whom Dante was a career-long inspiration) claimed that the *Vita Nuova* was anti-Romantic, teaching us not to expect more from life than it can give us and more from human beings than they can give, Williams hailed Dante as a theologian of Romantic Love and saw the *Commedia* as its scripture. He argued the relevance of relationships with other people as the source book for theological as well as literary interpretation. "We have looked everywhere for enlightenment on Dante," he wrote, "except in our lives and love-affairs." Conversely, "we ought perhaps to take Dante's poetry as relevant to our own affairs." To read the poet aright was to take lovers more seriously; it was to learn how to be " 'up to' Love" (*PD*, p. 27).

Williams wrote as someone schooled by Dante. Indeed, the experience of Beatrice – the theological erotic – was one that he knew very well, first in his relationship with the woman he married and then (although without sexual "knowledge") in his love for another woman.[5] He saw that romance per se was evanescent: like Beatrice herself in the *Vita Nuova*, it passes away. What matters most is what endures, what can be learned from that transfiguring passion and brought into the larger world of marriage, family, friendship, even the political order. The "Beatrician moment" reveals that the people we are given to love, and who occasionally love us back, can open us to the divine.

Williams believed that Dante did not impose theology on romance; rather, he understood that God was "imbedded" in all profound human loves, whether recognized as being there or not. Falling in love might be the beginning of a journey to God. If so, then "Look here! For I am Beatrice! I am!" becomes an invitation not only to pay attention to the beloved apart from one's own egotistical projections upon him or her, but also to pay attention to *everything* in the fullness of love.

The poet W. H. Auden counted Williams as a spiritual mentor. Moreover, he enlarged the presumed heterosexuality of the *Vita Nuova* and Williams's Romantic theology to include his own same-sex love: "When the Vision of Eros is genuine, I do not think it makes sense to apply to it terms like heterosexual or homosexual." In this opinion he was obviously reflecting on his own experience as someone whose Eros was same-sex. But he may also have had Dante in mind, for if the poet places sodomites in a circle of Hell reserved for those who committed "violence against nature" (*Inferno* 15–16), he also shows the purgatorial Terrace of Lust to be frequented by people we would call "gay" – and in equal number by those we would call "straight" – all going about the difficult business of refining their diverse erotic impulses. Auden doubted that the Vision of Eros (whatever its orientation) could long survive if the parties involved entered into an actual sexual relationship.[6] He saw a significant difference between the mountaintop and daily life below the peak. But he did not doubt the reality of the Vision. Plato had seen it first, and Dante had given it the name of "Beatrice."

Williams's *The Figure of Beatrice* was published a few years too late to have had a shaping hand in the way Auden launched his relationship with Chester Kallman shortly after the poet arrived in New York from Britain in 1939. In one form or another, the two men were companions until Auden's death in 1973. They had come together in the flesh, in a rough-and-tumble of excitement, disappointment, and jealousy that had nothing of the "sweet new style" about it. To think of Kallman as Auden's "Beatrice," at once gorgeous and chaste among the company of Heaven, would be an exercise in High Camp – the only imaginable response, gales of rude laughter. Moreover, even if Auden had hoped for monogamy with his lover, as he seems to have done in the beginning, he was soon disabused. Kallman was quite clearly not the man to provide for it, as Auden realized painfully in the autumn of 1941. Nor does it seem that either of them was much inclined, their homosexuality aside, to live up to the standards of Purgatory's "wives and husbands who were chaste, / as virtue and as matrimony mandate." Like most of us when it comes to our love lives, neither was worthy of emulation.

Nonetheless, it is difficult not to have both Dante and Williams's "Theology of Romantic Love" in mind when looking at a letter written by Auden to Kallman on Christmas Day 1941, after Kallman had a fling with someone else and, in sentimental terms, had broken Auden's heart.[7] Missing from the letter are the conventions of love lyrics that constitute the tradition sketched above: the unrequited passion of the lover, the untouchable beloved on a pedestal, the beloved's unexampled beauty and virtue. In this romance, everybody has feet of clay. But that this is a *love* letter is abundantly clear, not in spite of its warts-and-all approach but because of it. Clear, too, is the fact that its writer was someone, like Dante, for whom Eros and theology went hand-in-hand because in some sense, and on the deepest level, they were one.

In the letter, Auden takes the Christmas story and through each of its elements explores his affair with Kallman. The manger scene becomes not only the narrative backdrop but the interpretive key for their love. He begins by setting the stage and determining the rhetorical structure for what follows with a kind of logic: given X and Y, then Z:

> Because it is in you, a Jew, that I, a Gentile inheriting an
> O-so-genteel anti-semitism, have found my happiness;
>   As this morning I think of Bethlehem, I think of you.

He then continues, paragraph by paragraph, to give a fact about each of them that finds its clarification in the Gospel story. Because of who they are, in this way or that, the Nativity comes to life. Or to reverse the exchange, this or that aspect of their life together becomes intelligible through Scripture.

Because the Brooklyn boy has taught the Oxford snob that neither money nor education can buy love, Auden is reminded of the fact that Christ's Incarnation took place in the lowliness of the "inn stable." Because he has experienced the torments of sexual jealousy and has also known himself to be "in intention, and almost an act, a murderer," he thinks of the bloodthirsty King Herod. Kallman is to him "emotionally a mother, physically a father, and intellectually a son," and so the Holy Family comes to mind. Then, with what seems an explicit nod to the *Vita Nuova* and Williams's concept of the "Beatrician moment," "Because it is through you that God has chosen to show me my beatitude; / As this morning I think of the Godhead, I think of you."

In every paragraph, Auden grounds all his perceptions in "you," in Kallman, the quite specific person through whom his understanding of glory had embodied and revealed. This beloved is very much a "tu," not a "voi." "I think of you" is always the way he ends, giving thanks to the agent through whom the mystery came. But since Kallman was Kallman, and because "in the eyes of our bohemian friends our relationship is absurd," this love letter is laced with humor. The often unbearable seriousness of the courtly romance tradition finds here the occasion for a rueful grin or even for a joke. After all, human love is part of a divine *comedy*.

Auden ends with a pun, a "Grimm" prognosis for the future of the affair. Then his rhetoric ascends and he allows the all-too human to become sublime. In this final portion of the letter, furthermore, he makes it clear that it is not only the Nativity that has relevance to this love affair with Kallman: thinking of one part of Christ's story brings the rest along. Nor is there any limit to how the Incarnation can transfigure human relationships, even the most unlikely.

> Because our love, beginning Hans Christian Andersen, became Grimm, and there are probably even grimmer tests to come, nevertheless I believe that if only we have faith in God and in each other, we shall be permitted to realize all that love is intended to be;
>
> As this morning I think of the Good Friday and Easter Sunday implicit in Christmas day, I think of you.

We have no idea what Chester Kallman made of this letter any more than we know what Beatrice Portinari felt about the poet who dogged her on earth and followed her into the highest Heaven. In either case, however, the person writing the text believed that the personal love that "hit" him hard was intimately connected to the divine *amore* that "moves the sun and the other stars."

Chapter 4

Dante's Religion

It is commonplace to think of Dante as *the* Christian writer: medieval, Catholic, orthodox. This may be part of the picture, but not all. It neglects his idiosyncrasy, plays down the risks he took, and makes the whole enterprise of the *Commedia* a great deal more predictable (and less interesting) than it is. One of his great theological innovations, as we have seen, is Beatrice, a female Christ-figure. She should surprise Dante scholars more than she does; so too should much else that is strange in the poem – the presence of pagan adults in Limbo, for instance, or, more outrageous still, Dante's claim to have had the beatific vision of God while still a mortal.

What never fails to take readers aback, however, is Dante's attitude toward the Church of his day. Whereas one might well expect to find at least the polite respect for the Holy See we find today among even many nonbelievers, white-hot fury is what he shows the contemporary papacy. Popes get special "reserved seating" in Hell and an apoplectic denunciation by none other than St Peter. A loyal son of the Church, Dante nonetheless felt called to denounce what fell short of the gospel. There were "lawless shepherds" for instance, and a hierarchy in love with gold and silver. Furthermore, he felt free to make his harangue as a mere layman, with no authorization to speak as he did apart from his baptism and the passion of his convictions.

Dante's Core Beliefs

Given Dante's reputation as a "Christian Classic," it may seem that the core faith that informed his life was much like that of other medieval Catholics. This is very much the impression he wants to give – of someone fitting into the received faith rather than blazing trails. We see this most extensively in the theological examination the pilgrim takes in *Paradiso* 24–6, when one by one, Saints Peter, James, and John grill him on the three theological virtues (faith, hope, and charity or love). This three-canto sequence is patently an attempt to establish how far the pilgrim has come since his benighted thrashing about in the dark wood. It is also a well-timed occasion for the poet to pass the test of orthodoxy, colors flying, just before he makes the outrageous claim of seeing God "face to face." Whatever pushing of the envelope may be detected elsewhere, here the reader will find the author impeccable in his core beliefs. And so the meat-and-potato questions come fast and furious: what is faith, where did you get it, how much do you have?

In his surefire responses we see that Dante can quote Scripture and tradition with aplomb, demonstrating a skill in argumentation that would have stood him in good stead in the heady environment of the University of Paris. He does so with such panache that the disciples who formed Jesus's inner circle beam bright in their amazement. With them we watch him handle Scripture's "parchments old and new" (*Par.* 24.93), put the Creeds of the Church into his own words, and negotiate the peculiar reasoning ("sillogizzar," 24.77) of academic theology. "I believe in one God – sole, eternal," he tells St. Peter, "[and] in three Eternal Persons, / and these I do believe to be one essence, / so single and threefold as to allow / both *is* and *are*" (24.130, 139–41). All of this "faith," moreover, he holds like coins in his pocket. There is nothing for him to doubt – or, to translate the verb "s'inforsa" (l. 87) more literally, nothing "to perhaps about." Taken at face value this is a highly misleading claim: there is a great deal of "perhaps" in medieval theology and, more to the point, in Dante. But on the *basics* of Christian belief, no.

In his role as the pilgrim's examiner on this primary virtue, St Peter spins joyfully around him three times to celebrate so brilliant a performance (24.148–54). Then, without warning, the voice of the poet shatters the celebratory mood to speak about his own travail:

> If it should happen . . . If this sacred poem –
> this work so shared by heaven and by earth
> that it has made me lean through these long years –
> can ever overcome the cruelty
> that bars me from the fair fold where I slept,
> a lamb opposed to wolves that war on it,
> by then with other voice, with other fleece,
> I shall return as poet and put on,
> at my baptismal font, the laurel crown;
> for there I first found entry to that faith
> which makes souls welcome unto God, and then,
> for that faith, Peter garlanded my brow.
>
> (*Par.* 25.1–12)

There is much to observe in these lines, not the least of which is Dante's claim to be writing a "sacred poem" in which God has had a major hand. Then there is the dream of a return to Florence that by the time of this writing – close to his death, as it turns out – he knows will never take place. We also find a new vision of the city that until now he has so relentlessly blasted. Suddenly Florence is the beautiful sheepfold where he slept as a lamb. It is the place where he would be a faithful shepherd – enemy to ravening wolves – were not the city's gates barred against him. Finally, we sense his pride in what he has accomplished through his writing. He openly claims the title "poeta" until now reserved exclusively for the "greats" of classical antiquity: "ritornerò poeta," "I shall return as poet." Most telling, however, is the specific location where Dante wants to claim his laurel crown – the font where he was baptized. Everything should come together in the place where everything began: the great baptistery of Florence, with its towering program of mosaic iconography, in whose waters he became a Christian "welcome unto God."

Christian Florence

This, then, is the most basic answer to the question about the poet's belief: it was the faith "always and everywhere held" and, at least technically speaking, inaugurated in baptism. Dante would have received the sacrament on Easter Eve of 1266, almost a year after his birth – the ancient custom being to reserve baptisms of infants born during the previous year for that day in the Church year. His mention of this site adds more than local color to the passage: the baptistery of Florence, associated with the city's patron, St John the Baptist, looms large in his imagination, as indeed it did on the literal horizon of the city before the later construction of the present cathedral, the Duomo.

The poet mentions the baptistery in *Inferno* 19, in the context of a dramatic moment in his earlier life when he was forced to damage one of the fonts "in my handsome San

Giovanni" in order to save a life – "and let this be my seal to set men straight" (l. 21). We hear about the building again in *Paradiso* 25 when Dante's great-great-grandfather looks back to his own origins in twelfth-century Florence: "and I, within your ancient baptistery, / at once became Christian and Cacciaguida" (*Par.* 15.134–5).

Other holy places in Florence no doubt played their part in Dante's religious upbringing: the Alighieri family parish, San Martino Vescovo, and, at a later time, the great churches of the Mendicants or "begging" friars – the Franciscan Santa Croce and the Dominican Santa Maria Novella. There was also Santo Spirito, the Augustinian order's church.[1] We know from the *Convivio* that Dante had firsthand familiarity with at least two of these centers: to console himself for the death of Beatrice, for about two years he frequented "the schools of the religious and the disputations of the philosophers" (*Conv.* 2.12). The institutions referred to are the *studia generales* of the Mendicant orders, which together played the role of the university that Florence was not to have until the fifteenth century. Established primarily to train clerics, they also drew teachers and students from all over Europe. The *studia* were open to laypeople, at least in subjects like Scripture and theology. The dangers of science and philosophy were put off-limits to the laity – an interdiction which was made precisely because the "wrong people" were making their way in.

These centers of learning and piety offered different gifts. From the Augustinians at Santo Spirito, about whose *studium* little is known, Dante certainly came in contact with those two works of Augustine, namely the *Confessions* and the *City of God*, which play an important role in the *Commedia*. Among the Franciscans at Santa Croce Dante would have found not only the cult of St Francis of Assisi (d. 1226) but the legacies of Plato and Augustine, especially as filtered through the works of St Bonaventure (d. 1274). The teaching of Joachim of Fiore

Plate 1 Monika Beisner, *Inferno XIX*

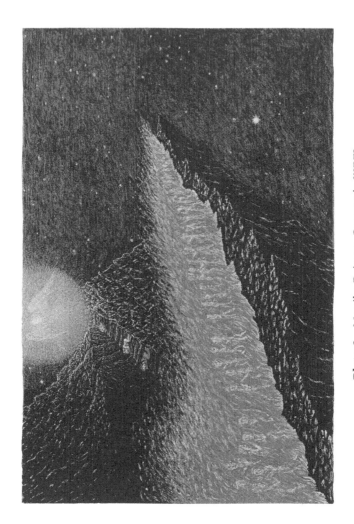

Plate 2 Monika Beisner, *Purgatorio XXVII*

Plate 3 Monika Beisner, *Paradies XVII*

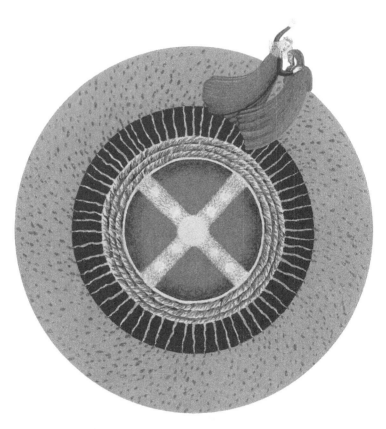

Plate 4   Monika Beisner, *Paradiso XVII*

(d. 1202) would also have been "in the air." We do not know if Dante personally heard great preachers like Petrus dell'Olivi, but his works show the influence of the Franciscan "Spiritualists," with their radical emphasis on the virtue of poverty, acute sense of crisis within the contemporary Church, and their apocalyptic expectation of a new age at hand. Franciscan preaching, following the animated spirit of the founder, typically reveled in narrative, drama, and emotion. The goal, as one preacher's manual had it, was to be "as agreeable as a jester and as sharp as a merchant."[2]

The followers of St Dominic (d. 1221), on the other hand, had a different style and other emphases: they turned to Aristotle and Thomas Aquinas (d. 1274), upheld intellectual rigor and a zeal for scholarship, had a greater openness to classical learning and the legacy of pagan Rome. They also appreciated the constructive possibilities of human reason. Dominican preachers delighted in intellectual argument, logic, and Scholastic methodology. Yet they could also be crowd-pleasers. Giordano da Pisa, for instance, thrilled congregations at Santa Maria Novella (in the years just following Dante's exile) not only with the weightier matters of science, philosophy, and theology but with "human interest" observations taken from everyday life.

Nor surprisingly, the Mendicants typically (though certainly not exclusively) appealed to different social and economic groups: the Franciscans to the humbler ranks of artisans, craftspeople, and shopkeepers; the Dominicans to an upper middle class of merchants, bankers, and lawyers.[3] Together they offered a richly diverse world of thought and sensibility not unlike Dante's own eclectic synthesis in the *Commedia*. The poet salutes the Mendicants in *Paradiso*'s Heaven of the Sun, where we find a celestial version of the "schools" blessedly free of the rivalry that in reality made these two different orders competitive if not openly antagonistic toward one another. Reflecting a goodwill practice observed on the feast days of Francis and Dominic, whereby a representative of one order praised the founder of the other in the rival's church, Dante brings the Mendicant world together in a celebration of harmony based on difference. In *Paradiso* 11, for instance, the Dominican Aquinas eulogizes St Francis; in canto 12, the Franciscan Bonaventure accords the same honor to St Dominic. Each theologian denounces the present-day corruption of his own community rather than finding fault with the other's. The effect of the sequence is to glorify mutuality, the concord of the one *and* the other: heart and intellect, the ardor of the seraph and the cherub's splendor (*Par.* 11:37–9), the call to poverty and the mandate to teach the faith.

In late thirteenth-century Florence, where literacy and religious devotion were uncommonly high among the laity, a person like Dante might join one of the *laudesi*, devotional groups that publicly sang praises (*laude*) to the Virgin Mary or one of the saints.[4] He could have chosen to belong to a charitable organization, called a *misericordia*, or joined one of the many penitential confraternities independent of the Mendicants but closely affiliated with them. An even closer connection with the Franciscans or Dominicans might be found in their tertiary or third orders, whereby the monastic communities attracted both men and women to the spiritual life. Although not bound by a vow to poverty or celibacy, whether privately in their own homes or communally with others, such people lived according to a voluntary rule. These groups had their impact on a hierarchy not otherwise benignly disposed to lay folks. A cardinal of the Church writing in 1255 observed that it was now possible "to use the term 'religious' for people who live in a holy and religious manner in their own homes, not because they are subject to a precise rule but because their life is simpler and more rigorous than that of other laypeople, who live in a purely worldly manner."[5]

Some have said that Dante meant to be a Franciscan in his youth but never took vows; others have imagined him a member of the Franciscan third order. (Despite the balance he accords these two "princes" of the Church – one canto is devoted to each in the Heaven of the Sun [*Par.* 10–14] – the scale effectively tips toward Francis.) Whatever the case, Dante was probably among the many who flocked to the great churches of the Franciscans and Dominicans, where laypeople could discover an intensity of Christian life not found in the ordinary parish. Preaching was at the center of this experience. Lay people gathered en masse in the new piazzas, great open spaces built in front of the churches to accommodate their numbers. Conversely, they might meet together in the more intimate setting of a confraternity.

In one sense, the goal of the monks in their outreach to this urban population was catechesis. They wanted to teach the faith to an increasingly sophisticated populace, to bring about the conversion of nominal believers into deeper (more orthodox) Catholics. As part of this goal, they translated their clerical training into forms that might be accessible to laypeople. Their effort was to turn the Latin erudition of the schools and devotional spirit of the cloister into a spiritual vernacular able to speak to the realities of secular life. Dante learned much from their project: indeed, in so many regards it became his own in the *Commedia*.

A Personal Faith Story

Apart from conjectures about Dante's Christian formation, is it possible to discover in his work any sense of his personal experience of religion? The answer is "Yes." Looking at his writing from start to finish, there seems to be a spiritual autobiography in the making – an extended drama of conversion, falling away, and reconversion that joins his *Vita Nuova* to the exilic writing of the *Convivio* and *Commedia*. From the beginning, Dante's theology of Romantic love centered on Beatrice. She was his baptism into the experience of love, so that through her he "first found entry to that faith which makes souls welcome unto God" (*Par.* 25.10–11). His subsequent turn to Lady Philosophy in the *Convivio* – his putting away of childish things in favor of knowledge as the way to perfection – is his response to the wreckage of his public and private life. In exile he seeks the consolation of philosophy and takes "her" to be his beloved.

Dante's unfinished *Convivio* is a celebration of the human desire for knowledge, "in which our supreme happiness is found" (*Conv.* 1.1). The opening book warns that there are obstacles to moving on this path: immersion in evil, physical incapacity, absorption in practical duties, and sheer laziness. Nonetheless, the work as a whole argues that the quest for knowledge is within reach, even for those Latin "illiterates" who can only find their philosophy, thanks to him, in Italian. One dedicated to wisdom can, with struggle, attain the goal. Intellect gives rise to faith, and faith to hope, and hope to charity: "Through these three virtues men rise to philosophize in that heavenly Athens towards which, through the dawning of eternal truth, the Stoics, the Peripatetics and the Epicureans hasten together, united in the harmony of a single will" (3.14).

This confidence fell apart in the course of whatever personal breakdown is represented by the dark wood of *Inferno* 1. Philosophy ultimately could not satisfy him. In this he was like St Augustine, who turned to "the books of the Platonists" for a time – and never lost their influence – but finally could not find comfort or fulfillment in their ancient version of self-help. From the later perspective of the *Commedia*, moreover, this turn from one "lady" to another constitutes a loss of faith, an abandonment of the true way. The *Commedia* insists on the pilgrim's helplessness, and it is definitely not Philosophy who comes to his rescue but the intercession of the Virgin Mary and the whole company of Heaven standing behind the interventions of Beatrice and Virgil. Dante by no means loses respect for philosophy: the *Commedia* is inconceivable without it. But from the poem's dramatic beginning onward, human knowledge and will are shown to be hopeless without the power of grace. The "heavenly Athens" of Stoics, Peripatetics, and Epicureans is only Limbo, the first circle of Hell. It is beautiful, refined, civil, and dead. Knowledge may well be perfection, but it is the knowledge *of God*, the beatific vision, that is the journey's true end. That vision is a gift to be received, not acquired. No one can read his or her way into enlightenment. Instead, love must find a way.

But Where is Christ?

Beatrice, as we have seen, is Dante's particular understanding of "the way, the truth, and the life" (John 14:6); she is his "Christ event." But what about the Savior himself? A Dante student once confided his dismay over what he called the "surprising absence" of Christ from the *Divine Comedy*.[6] He acknowledged that the poem offered a panoramic Christian vision; he also saw that the *Paradiso* moved the pilgrim from one saintly encounter to another. Surely some kind of meeting with the Savior was bound to take place. Yet there was none, at least there was nothing remotely like what one would expect to find in an early fourteenth-century text written by a poet who so deeply venerated St Francis. It was Francis, after all, who gave western Christianity a new understanding of the Incarnation as vulnerably human; and Francis who became the suitor of Lady Poverty after Christ made her a widow with his death on the cross (*Par*. 11.64–72). Out of the saint's personal piety came the cult of the infant's crib at Bethlehem, as well as devotion to the Man of Sorrows, who bore in his very human body all the pain that flesh is heir to. Indeed, Francis's entire vocation unfolded before the image of the Crucified, first in the ruined chapel of San Damiano, when the crucifix told him "Rebuild my Church," and finally on Mount L'Averna, where he received the wounds of Christ, the *stigmata*, in his own body.

Yet Francis's intimacy with the divine, not to mention the Franciscan focus on the incarnate Son of Man, is decidedly not what we find in the *Commedia*. Until Dante's rapture takes place in the closing lines of the poem, God the Blessed Trinity of Father, Son, and Holy Spirit is known only second-hand, and as reflected in the many triune structures of the poem: three canticles, three realms of the afterlife, the building block of the tercet's triple lines, the rhyme scheme of *terza rima*. Or God is spoken about by the souls who tell what they can about the One in whom they live, move, and have their being. Among these are Piccarda, "in His will is our peace" (*Par.* 3.85); Cacciaguida, "Blessed are you, both Three and One, who show / such favor to my seed" (*Par.* 15.47–8), and St Bernard of Clairvaux, "The King through whom this kingdom finds content . . . bestows His grace diversely, at His pleasure – and here the fact alone must be enough" (*Par.* 32. 61, 65–6). Divinity is disclosed indirectly, and with few revelations that depart from received Catholic doctrine. Only at the very end of this prolonged mediation does the incarnate Christ come into focus for a split second – his face Dante's last sight before being caught up into the beatific vision.

The Christ of the Theologians

For all this indirection, there is nonetheless one moment in the *Commedia* – in *Paradiso* 7 – when Beatrice speaks directly about Christ in a careful theological exposition of why the Word of God chose to redeem humanity by becoming flesh. She speaks of these heady matters in response to the pilgrim's unvoiced question: why did God choose precisely *this* pathway for our redemption (ll. 56–7)? Her answer, delivered in the mode of a Scholastic Master of Theology, is a composite of St Anselm's eleventh-century treatise, *Cur Deus Homo?* ("Why did God become Man?"), and of Thomas Aquinas in *Summa Theologiae* 3, 46–50. The poet is happy to reveal what he knows, and once again to acknowledge his debt to authority. According to this well-rehearsed line of reasoning, only God could possibly repair the breach made by Adam between the divine and the human. Yet rather than simply cancel the original sin, God chose instead the "so magnificent procedure" (l. 113) of the Incarnation. The first Adam had reached high in his disobedient pride, but the second Adam, the Son of God, descended even lower in humility by taking on our flesh. In this act, God showed himself to be both abundantly merciful and supremely just:

> for God showed greater generosity
> in giving His own self that man might be
> able to rise, than if He simply pardoned;
>   for every other means fell short of justice,
> except the way whereby the Son of God
> humbled Himself when He became incarnate.
>
> (*Par.* 7.115–20)

Here, as elsewhere in the *Paradiso*, Dante chooses one possible theological position over another. He parts ways with the Franciscan philosopher and theologian Duns Scotus (d. 1308), who held that, even if Adam and Eve had never fallen, the Incarnation would have taken place. Dante by contrast emphasizes not the inevitability of the Word made flesh, but, rather, God's choice to become human: "the Son of God / humbled himself when He became incarnate." The poet's parsing of the mystery is clear, distinct, largely purified of metaphor; it is also devoid of any particular originality. As in his theological examination in *Paradiso* 24–6, Dante shows us that he can "talk the talk" with the best of the masters. The otherwise audacious poet steps aside to allow theological tradition to speak. Except, of course, that tradition normally "speaks" in Latin, not Italian, and through ordained men, not a Florentine laywoman! This is tradition with a difference.

Mediations of Christ in the Commedia

Beatrice's magisterial discussion of the Savior's redemption is not typical of how an otherwise "absent" Christ appears in the poem. In fact, rather than referring to his *absence* from the *Commedia*, we would do better to speak of his refracted presence within it. One way to see the poem is as an extended journey into the mystery of the Incarnation, with each of the three canticles offering an encounter with the Word-made-flesh that accords with its particular mode of vision and poetic representation: the parodic, the symbolic, and the unmediated.

We begin in Hell's "region of unlikeness" where evil appears as a twisted manifestation of the Good. Inferno is scarred by reminiscences of Christ's descent among the dead, with Hell's gates shattered, its walls cracked and crumbling. (In *Paradiso*, these infernal memories will be supplemented with recalls of the eclipse that took place on Golgotha.) On Good Friday afternoon 1300 Dante follows in Christ's footsteps, descending into the kingdom of death and witnessing everywhere the travesty of the ruined image of God in myriad contorted forms. At the "bottom of the universe" (recall

Chapter 2), he comes upon the frozen carcass of Satan. A seraph's pure spirit becomes a gargantuan Incarnation. His single head sprouts a trio of faces, and his transfixed body serves Dante as a grotesque ladder or "scala" (*Inf.* 34.82, 119) leading him up and out of Hell. In this way, Satan's flesh serves in the same capacity as Christ's cross – an exit from sin and death, a horrible but effective access to the light.

Satan is what the Incarnation looks like in the "sorrowful kingdom" (*Inf.* 34.28). When the union of spirit and flesh is beheld on the top of Mount Purgatory, however, it takes on another aspect and becomes a different kind of mediation. *Purgatorio* is the realm of metaphor and symbol, not parody. It is full of dreams that convey enigmatic truth, a place where the literal becomes figurative. Take the griffin that appears at the center of Eden's Pageant of Revelation in *Purgatorio* 29 – "the beast which is one sole person in two natures" (*Purg.* 31.80–1). At first look, Dante sees the griffin as a physical composite, half eagle, half lion. But when he stares into Beatrice's unveiled eyes and sees the griffin mirrored there – that is, when he looks into the eyes of the woman who had been the Christ Event in his own life – he sees something stranger still. The griffin appears first in the guise of one of his natures and then in the other:

> Just like the sun within a mirror, so
> the double-natured creature gleamed within,
> now showing one, and now the other guise.
> Consider, reader, if I did not wonder
> when I saw something that displayed no movement
> though its reflected image kept on changing.
>
> (*Purg.* 31.121–6)

The effect is uncanny, like the familiar Gestalt example of the rabbit-duck. The eye can take in one or the other, but not the two at once. So here: the griffin is a Gestalt of the Incarnation, seen as an eagle at one instance and a lion at another. The point is not that one of these representations "stands for" Christ's humanity and the other for his divinity; it is to demonstrate the impossibility of holding in mind at one and the same time the two natures in one Person. When the lion changes into the eagle, the eagle into the lion, we are meant to "see" what cannot be shown. As the Nicene Creed has it, he is "very God of very God" *and* "born of the Virgin Mary and made man."

In the final stage of the poem's itinerary, the types and shadows of *Purgatorio* give way to *Paradiso*'s unmediated vision. At least, this is the poetic fiction of the final canticle: Dante, in fact, is doomed to use the temporal medium of language to articulate the ineffable. The poem is always an "as if" rather than an "is." Still, words may imply what they cannot say, and visible things *almost* disappear into the invisible reality they attempt to represent.

At the very end of the *Paradiso*, the poet finally gives us what we have been gradually moving toward. After Satan's parody of God and the griffin's allegory of Christ's two natures we arrive at an unfolding vision of the Triune God. First, a convergence of the multiform universe into a single knot of reality likened to a volume bound by love. Then, three circles of equal dimension distinguished one from the other by three different colors.

> one circle seemed reflected by the second,
> as rainbow is by rainbow; and the third
> seemed fire breathed equally by those other two circles.
>
> (Par. 33.118–20)

Gazing on this manifestation of the Trinity, Dante finds his attention suddenly caught by the appearance of something new ("quella vista nova," l. 136). Imprinted on the central circle of the three he sees our human image and likeness, "la nostra effige" (l. 131). At last, the face of Christ!

The pilgrim ponders the ultimate mystery of God and tries to understand how it is that Christ's flesh could ever "in-where itself" ("s'indova," l. 138) in the uncreated Trinity. In this longing to "figure out" the Incarnation he is, we are told, like a geometer working with all his might to square the circle. The effort fails even as the poem comes rapidly to a conclusion that is just short of its goal "to see the way in which our human effigy suited the circle and founds its place in it" (ll. 136–8). Yet this failure is no cause for regret, for in the final lines of the final canto Dante's intellect is enraptured by the love that moves the sun and the other stars. The mystery of the God he could not solve takes him over. In this rush of visionary events, and before Dante's blackout into God's light, his final vision is the human face of the second Person of the Trinity. It is from Christ's visage, then, that he moves "face to face" into the beatific vision of a God.

Mary as Christ's Flesh

In this way the *Commedia* ends "in Christ." Yet when the poet wants Christological doctrine to sing, when he wants to give the reader some *feeling* for the Word-made-flesh, he shifts from the typology of the Old and New Adam he relied on in *Paradiso* 7, and along with it the abstract language of formal theology. He turns instead to the Blessed Virgin Mary. This move should come as no surprise (even if it disappoints the diehard Protestant) given Mary's extraordinary prominence in the poem: she is the one who initiates Dante's rescue from the dark wood and ultimately directs his gaze to the vision of the Trinity. Hers is the name, as the poet tells us in *Paradiso* 23, "which I always

/ invoke, at morning and at evening" (ll. 88–9). In addition, Mary provides the focus for Dante's most affective presentation of Christ's Incarnation. She is the "way" whereby the second Adam redeemed the first Adam's sin. God the Son raised up humanity by humbling himself, but it was Mary who provided the medium for that magnificent "humiliation" – who gave God *our* flesh.

Whereas other contemporaries celebrated the bloody wounds of the stigmata or entered meditatively into Christ's physical suffering, Dante presents us with Mary's inviolate body – her womb, her breasts, her smile. For whatever auto-biographical reason, be it psychological or experiential, it is through female mediation that he comes to know God in the poem, and through Mary that he finally enters into Christ. The emotional drama of the Incarnation is played out through her, so that in order to know Jesus of Nazareth you must look to the source of his flesh, to his mother. Or, to recall the Catholic mantra of yore, one goes "to Jesus through Mary."

Indeed, it is *her* experience of Christ – reported so sparely in the Gospels – that becomes Dante's way of showing us the events of the Redeemer's earthly life. We recall his Nativity by remembering that she suffered the pangs of childbirth (*Purg.* 3.39); we experience his Passion by recalling her bitter weeping at the foot of the cross (*Purg.* 33.6), quite as much as by remembering Christ crying out "*Eli*" (*Purg.* 23.74). The "Quest for the Historical Jesus," in other words, leads us to the Life of Mary. *Her* footsteps are the ones we are meant to follow on the Way of the Cross.

This is seen most clearly along the purgatorial terraces, where penitents are constantly reminded (in imagery, vision, or song) of Mary's intimate knowledge of her son: her presentation of the baby Jesus in the Jerusalem Temple; her loss of him when he is about his "father's business" among the teachers of the Law; her asking him to see about the wine at the wedding in Cana; and the moment on Golgotha when she stands at the foot of his cross. To enrich these recollections Dante might easily have drawn upon the wealth of legendary stories that were devised in the Middle Ages to help fill in the blanks of the Virgin's scant biblical story.[7] Of all Dante's Marian recollections, however, it is the Annunciation, represented on both the first (10.34–45) and the last of the purgatorial terraces (25.128), that touches him most deeply.

Inscribed in the wall of the Terrace of Pride is a tableau reminiscent of countless medieval carvings, paintings, and manuscript illuminations. We see the sudden appearance of the angel, the startled young woman, the dialogue (Luke 1: 26–38) that changes history. Dante emphasizes the scripted or "storiated" aspect of his presentation by having the silent picture he describes seem to speak the Latin text of the Vulgate translation of the Bible. In iconography this was done by having the words of Scripture scroll out of a figure's mouth, much like the balloon speech of a contemporary comic strip.

> The angel who reached earth with the decree
> of that peace which, for many years, had been
> invoked with tears, the peace that opened Heaven
>   after long interdict, [that angel] appeared before us,
> his gracious action carved with such precision –
> he did not seem to be a silent image.
>   One would have sworn that he was saying, "*Ave!*";
> for in that scene there was the effigy
> of one who turned the key that had unlocked
>   the highest love; and in her stance there were
> impressed these words, "*Ecce ancilla Dei*,"
> precisely like a figure stamped in wax.
>   (*Purg.* 10.34–45)

This portrait of humility gives us the starting point of the Incarnation when Mary's "Yes" allowed the divine Word to become flesh. Venerable ways of reading the Bible "under-write" the scene. Just as the second Adam redeemed the disobedience of the first, so Mary rewrites the Fall of human-kind to become the New Eve. This transformation is encoded within Gabriel's greeting: "Ave!" rewrites the tangled legacy of "Eva" and turns a fallen name into praise. Likewise, Gabriel brings peace to earth after long enmity, reversing the work of the angels in Genesis 3:24 who with flaming swords guarantee that Paradise is truly lost once God expels Adam and Eve from Eden.

Most telling for Dante's presentation of humility in this tableau is the emphasis placed on Mary's activity in the Annunciation story, on her *agency*. Although represented in the stance of a handmaid, she is nonetheless God's partner in redemption: it is she who changes the course of human his-tory. From the time of the Fall, the door to Heaven had been shut tight, the earth punished under divine interdict. But then Mary took hold of the key that God placed in her hand. She turned the lock, opened the door, and released the "highest love" that had been waiting to come down. In this moment, the handmaid of the Lord became the Mother of God.

The Annunciation seen in *Purgatorio* 10 gives us our first sight of Mary, placed on the threshold of the Incarnation, nine months before Christ's birth. But when the Virgin appears for the first time in her own right – not as the anonymous "lady in Heaven" of *Inferno* 2's flashback or in these many purgatorial representations – she does so, however momentarily, in the company of her son. This appearance takes place in *Paradiso* 23, when Dante and Beatrice ascend to the Heaven of the Fixed Stars and the pilgrim is afforded a "preview" of the court of Heaven: Christ, Mary, and "the ancient and the new council" of Hebrews and Christians (l. 138). The Church Triumphant itself appears alternately as a vast multitude of flames and as a meadow of light. Here too the work of mediation continues, for the pilgrim is not yet ready to see the blessed in the resurrection bodies they will assume in the Empyrean. Reality still wears the masquerade of metaphor. And so the Son of God appears as a sun that blazes above the "fair garden blossoming beneath Christ's rays" (l. 72); the blessed are "the lilies / whose fragrance let men find the righteous way" (ll. 74–5); and Mary (identified by the flower she shares with Venus, goddess of love) is "the rose in which the Word of God became flesh" (ll. 73–4). By the end of the poem this single Marian rose will become Heaven itself: the City of God appears as a "candida rosa" (*Par.* 31.1), white with a golden center, and in perpetual bloom. Thus the blessed are (to introduce a neologism Dante might well have composed) in-Mary-ed.

Dante's immediate impulse in *Paradiso* 23 is to look directly at the Christ-sun that makes the celestial garden "in-flower itself" ("s'infiora," l. 72); but his "lucent Substance" is simply too overpowering. And for good reason, says Beatrice:

> "What overwhelms you is a Power
> against which nothing can defend itself.
>   This is the Wisdom and the Potency
> that opened roads between the earth and Heaven,
> the paths for which desire had since long waited."
>
> (*Par.* 23.35–49)

The identification of Christ as the "power and wisdom of God" is biblical (1 Cor. 1:24); the notion of the Redeemer as a conqueror who cannot be resisted also recalls the story of the Harrowing of Hell, when Christ battered down the gates of Hades and liberated those who long desired his coming. At this point in the journey, the pilgrim cannot look upon a Christ who is still too blindingly bright. Nonetheless, Dante *can* behold Mary, the next brightest light in this heaven – the one who opened the door of Heaven and gave God the flesh whereby he might be seen, touched, and listened to.

At the end of *Paradiso* 23, Dante watches as Mary is crowned by Gabriel, messenger of the Annunciation. The archangel circles her head and in doing so spins a garland of light. We are told that his joy is inspired by ''the womb / that was the dwelling place of our Desire'' (ll. 104–5). Yet it is not only Mary's womb, the ''inn'' where heavenly desire rested for nine months, that we are asked to consider in this appearance; there is also her arms' embrace and the succor of her breasts. As mother follows her son into the Empyrean at the end of *Paradiso* 23, the flames concealing each of the blessed flicker after her, all of them caught in an updraft of affection. Dante interprets this sputtering of heavenly fire as a sure sign of their devotion. It occasions one of the more poignant likenesses in the entire poem.

> And like an infant who, when it has taken
> its milk, extends its arms out to its mother,
> its feeling kindling into outward flame,
>   so each of those blessed splendors stretched its peak
> upward, so that the deep affection each
> possessed for Mary was made plain to me.
>
> (*Par.* 23.121–6)

Mary is the *Mater Ecclesiae*, Mother of the Church, and therefore the blessed who swell the ranks of the Church Triumphant are all her offspring. They are joined to her as mother and through her, to Christ her son. Yet what makes the likeness so startling is how it transposes the court of Heaven into a nursery, and turns Mary into a wetnurse.

Infantile bliss is not the poet's only way of imagining beatitude. At the close of the *Paradiso*, Dante will present the heavenly city not only as a white rose but also as a massive work of architecture – an imperial amphitheater presided over by a Queen of Heaven who is called empress, "Agusta" (32.119). In this presentation we find a magnificent forum filled with courtiers and as close to a fulfillment of Dante's imperial dream as he will ever get. But earlier, in the foretaste of the City of God given in *Paradiso* 23, the poet places us in a radically different metaphoric context – a mother's womb and breast, with nursing infants who suck their fill and afterwards are flush with pleasure

Dante does not directly offer a Madonna and Child, as did countless Italian painters before and after his poem. In *Paradiso* we are looking only at lights, thinking about flowers, and likening the ardor of the saints to the love of children for their mother. Nonetheless, Dante's readers would have understood that the only child Mary actually nursed was the Son of God. The poet moves our understanding of the Incarnation quite beyond the abstract theological terms of *Paradiso* 7, in whose theological account Mary plays no role at all. There we were mindful of the Second Adam's arduous redemption of the First; here we feel an infant's pleasure in being fed. We imagine the Word made flesh as a tiny child, full of mother's milk, awash in tenderness.

In the last four cantos of the *Commedia* Dante pretends to abandon metaphor in order to give us an unmediated vision of the real. St Bernard of Clairvaux replaces Beatrice as guide: he names names and points out individual faces within the City of God. As in Bernard's earthly life, so too in eternity he is the *alumnus familiarissimus Dominae Nostrae*, "the most intimate nursling of Our Lady" (as described by Pope Alexander III at Bernard's canonization in 1173). His devotion is entirely concentrated on the Virgin Mary, on "the face that is most like / the face of Christ" (32. 85–6), the one "whose semblance was so akin to God (l. 93). Like mother, like son.

Following Bernard's bidding, Dante lifts his gaze and witnesses yet another re-enactment of the Annunciation. The archangel Gabriel hovers above the Virgin, leading the entire court of Heaven – Hebrews and Gentiles, saints and angels – in singing *Ave Maria, gratïa plena*. These words were first spoken by the angel in Nazareth, in the last minutes of the Old dispensation; now they are sung in Heaven to celebrate the young woman who opened a door on the New. Yet even in the full flush of Marian devotion, Dante reminds us that the angel's song ultimately has Christological meaning. Mary's ''Yes'' to God came as a response to God's ''Yes'' to humanity in Christ. The instant she agreed to offer her womb to her Creator, says Bernard, was the moment ''when God's Son / wanted to bear our flesh as His own burden'' (32.113–14).

Daughter of Her Son

It is to the God-bearer, the giver of the burden, that Bernard turns at the opening of the poem's 100th canto, asking Mary to strengthen Dante for a face-to-face encounter with her son. His prayer begins as follows:

> ''Virgin mother, daughter of your Son,
> more humble and sublime than any creature,
> fixed goal decreed from all eternity,
>   you are the one who gave to human nature
> so much nobility that its Creator
> did not disdain His being made its creature.
>   That love whose warmth allowed this flower to bloom
> within the everlasting peace – was love
> rekindled in your womb.''

> (*Par.* 33.1–9)

In this beautiful set piece we are asked to confront the mystery of the Incarnation in the person of one who is celebrated as God's *termine fisso*, as the "fixed goal decreed from all eternity." Dante allows the sublime eloquence of the historical Bernard's hymns, sermons, and commentary on the Song of Songs to echo throughout these lines; so too do the words of such authorities as Ambrose (d. 397), Bonaventure (d. 1274), and Peter Damian (d. 1072). Again, the poet reveals his Latin reading at the same time that he transforms it into vernacular rhyme.

Faced with so divine a mystery, however, eloquence tumbles into sublime nonsense. Reason throws up its hands before the Incarnation and language takes refuge in paradox. Antitheses collide, opposites coincide. The virgin is not only a mother but the daughter of her son; lowliness is height; the Creator becomes a creature, and a woman's flesh blossoms into divine light. No less a student of Dante than T. S. Eliot may well have had these lines in mind in his *Four Quartets*, when he too strains to give an account of "the intersection of the timeless with time":

> The hint half guessed, the gift half understood, is Incarnation.
> Here the impossible union
> Of spheres of existence is actual,
> Here the past and future
> Are conquered, and reconciled
>
> ("The Dry Salvages," 5.32–6)

Mary receives Bernard's words with a smile, and then turns upward to the divine light that transcends even her luminosity. Dante follows her gaze straight into the heart of the Trinity, where he sees the face that most resembles Mary's and recognizes in its features our human likeness.

St Bonaventure described this movement from a vision of the incarnate Christ to the direct experience of the Godhead in the final chapter of his *Itinerarium Mentis in Deum,* a book that Dante knew well. Christ is "the way and the door...the stairway and the vehicle," and it is by meditating on him that the contemplative abandons all mental operations. Once that happens, he or she finds that human affection is "transformed and transferred into God": "with Christ crucified let us pass out of this world to the Father."[8] But whereas Bonaventure made this journey into the ineffable by looking upon the Crucified, nailed and suspended from the cross, Dante instead focuses on the power of the resurrection in the bosom of the Trinity. The pilgrim's final vision is of the *glory* of the Incarnation. He beholds a mother's son – Mary's flesh suffused with God's light.

The Beatific Smile

But what is it exactly that Dante sees when he looks into that divine face? We are not told that any particular expression plays across "la nostra effige" (*Par.* 33.131). The abstraction generally favored by the *Paradiso,* and the extreme sublimity of the moment, argue against it. If we imagine anything, it is the traditional icon's bold impassive stare. Yet the poet hints that a smile might be exactly what Dante sees. The idea is outlandish, but no more so than Dante's praise of God in the poem's final canto, as One who smiles upon himself:

> Eternal Light, You only dwell within
> Yourself, only You know You, Self-knowing,
> Self-known, You love and smile upon Yourself!
> *(Par.* 33. 124–6)

It is Trinitarian commonplace to speak of the Divine Persons knowing and loving each other. The distinctive *Dantean* touch, however, is found in the notion of a self-reflecting divine smile, of God as a community of eternal, spontaneous delight. In this regard Dante is like Meister Eckhart (d. 1327), a contemporary to the North, who understood that "When the Father laughs at the Son and the Son laughs back at the Father, that laughter gives pleasure, that pleasure gives joy, that joy gives love, and that love is the Holy Spirit."[9] Given this mutual joy, this triune smiling, it would not be out of keeping if the divine face that Dante beholds at the very end of his vision were quite specifically marked by a smile.

Because of the ongoing popularity of the *Inferno* at the expense of the other two canticles, most people identify the poet and his religion with the horrors of Hell. It is as if a vision of damnation were Dante's great contribution to the Christian imagination – as if he were, in fact, Nietzsche's savage caricature of him as a "hyena who writes poetry in tombs."[10] The truth is quite the contrary, *if* one takes in the whole of the *Commedia*. For what Dante has given the tradition is a notion that joy is at the heart of reality, even at the heart of God. Smiling, moreover, is the hallmark gesture of Dante's poem and a sign of his distinctiveness as both poet and theologian.

Sorriso/sorridere and *riso/ridere* – either as noun or verb, and apparently meaning interchangeably "smile" or "laugh" – appear over 70 times in the poem, and in a wide variety of contexts. The first instance is near the beginning of *Inferno*, as Virgil smiles upon Dante in Limbo when the great poets of antiquity turn to the pilgrim with a sign of greeting, welcoming him as one of their own (*Inf.* 4.99). In the following canto, Francesca recalls that single moment in the Lancelot romance when the "longed-for smile" of Guinevere – her "disïato riso" (5.133) – draws the knight into her embrace, and Paolo and Francesca to their doom. Thereafter, smiling is reserved exclusively for the province of redemption: over 20 instances in the *Purgatorio* and more than double that number in the *Paradiso*.

Occasionally, the smile appears on a cosmic scale: at various points we are told that Venus (*Purg.* 1.20), the Moon (*Par.* 23.26), Mercury (5.97), Mars (14.86), and Jupiter (20.13) all prompt a smile, a dazzle of joyful light, in the heavens. These local expressions are surpassed in *Paradiso* 27 when Dante's successful completion of his three-part theological examination provokes "un riso / del universo" (ll. 4–5), "a smile of the universe." The poet likens this joyful brightening to the sudden clearing of a misty sky, "so that the heavens smile with loveliness in all their regions" (28.83–4).

Often, however, smiling emphasizes a distinctly *human* connection between the dead and the living – a bond of easy affection that works against the tragic failed embrace that Dante found in Virgil's epic tradition. In the "waiting room" of Ante-Purgatory, for instance, Casella (2.83) and Manfred (3.112) both smile upon seeing Dante appear in their temporary way station of the afterlife. It is the pilgrim's turn to grin when he discovers that Belacqua, in word and deed, is still his lazy old self (4.122). Samuel Beckett in *The Lost Ones* says that this meeting "wrung from Dante one of his rare wan smiles."[11] The Beckett Archive in Reading University, England, includes a note card that keeps score of such moments. But there is no reason to assume anything wan about the encounter with Belacqua – or about any of the others that follow in the *Purgatorio*.

Indeed, the smiles exchanged in the second canticle contribute as much to Purgatory's new atmosphere of light, color, and emotional warmth as the rediscovered presence of the sun. After his sojourn on the Terrace of Pride, Dante discovers by touch that there are now only six remaining "P"s (each signifying a *peccatum* or one of the deadly sins) on his forehead.

Virgil openly enjoys the sight: ''and as he watched me do this, my guide smiled'' (12.136). He does so once again as the pilgrim passes through the refining fire of lust on the final terrace, lured through the flames by one Virgilian blandishment after another: ''then [he] smiled / as one smiles at a child fruit has beguiled'' (27.44–5).

The encounter with Statius in *Purgatorio* 21, moreover, is a veritable profusion of heartfelt smiles. Hearing Statius praise Virgil to the skies, but enjoined to keep the master's identity concealed, Dante struggles against the flash of a smile – ''un lampeggiar di riso'' (l. 114) – that he cannot quite conceal and must in the end explain: ''Ancient spirit, you / perhaps are wondering at the smile I smiled: / but I would have you feel still more surprise'' (ll. 121–3). The Statius episode is not only the scene of smiles first suppressed and then expressed; it is also a stimulus for our own smiling. In my experience, no reader of *Purgatorio* 21 fails to mimic the textual ''lampeggiar di riso.''

Higher up on the purgatorial mountain, Matelda is all smiles within the Garden of Eden (28.67, 76, 96). When she suggests that the ancient poets who sang of the Golden Age might actually have dreamed of this very place ''and its happy state,'' Virgil and Statius take her words as a compliment to their kind. They acknowledge her gracious ''corollary'' to them with a spontaneous grin: ''Then I turned around completely and I faced / my poets,'' says Dante, ''I could see that they had heard / with smiles this final corollary spoken'' (ll.145–7).

At the climactic moment of the pilgrim's reunion with Beatrice, her unveiling, we are not told precisely how she looks at him, but surely it can only be a smile that breaks forth when the lady uncovers not only her ''holy eyes'' but also the ''second beauty'' of her mouth (*Purg.* 31.133–45). What Dante beholds on her face is both her individual joy and her reflection of God's light:

> O splendor of eternal living light,
> who's ever grown so pale beneath Parnassus'
> shade or has drunk so deeply from its fountain,
>   that he'd not have his mind confounded,
> trying to render you as you appeared
> where heaven's harmony was your pale likeness –
>   your face, seen through the air, unveiled completely?
>   (*Purg.* 31.139–45)

Finally, when Dante protests after his immersion in the river Lethe that he does not recall ever making himself a stranger to Beatrice (33.91–102), the lady responds to him not with a barbed reproach but with a smile (l. 95). It is a holy version of the one she used to flash at him on earth: "with its old net, / the holy smile so drew [my eyes] to itself" (32.5–6). With the machinery of courtly love – the repertoire of eyes and mouth, the "old net" of physical beauty – Beatrice's smile still "works" in the context of Heaven's *vita nuova*.

Beatrice continues to radiate in this way throughout the *Paradiso*. Sometimes it is out of impatience or in amusement over Dante's incomprehension of beatitude (e.g., 1.95, 2.52, 3.24–5). Likewise Piccarda in the Heaven of the Moon: she first appears with eyes smiling ("con occhi ridenti," 3.42) and then goes on to "smile a little" (l. 67) when Dante wonders if she might be happier in some more exalted place. More often, the blessed are experienced by the pilgrim (and signified by the poet) as coruscations of light, or quite simply *as* smiles: Justinian (5.126), Gratian (10.103), Orosius (10.118), Thomas Aquinas (11.17), and Cacciaguida, who is said to be "at once hidden and revealed by his smile" (17.36). (The contemporary reader must struggle to put out of mind both the Cheshire Cat of John Tenniel's *Alice in Wonderland* illustrations and the ubiquitous "Happy Face" that is currently "all smiles" wherever we look.)

Beatrice's "dolce riso" appears again and again as an expression of joy over Dante's spiritual progress. Because the light that flashes from her eyes and mouth is a quintessence of Paradise, she can dazzle and overwhelm. Thus the pilgrim speaks of her "conquering my will with her smile's splendor" (18.19). On one occasion she even withholds this expression of tenderness and joy that customarily lifts Dante to a higher celestial sphere. Not wanting him to become like Semele, incinerated on beholding Jove in his divinity, she refuses to smile in the Heaven of Saturn (21.4–12). Yet just two cantos later, in the Heaven of the Fixed Stars, Dante is able to do more than withstand Beatrice's "santo riso" (23.59); he is able, by invitation, to take it all in:

> "Open your eyes and see what I now am;
> the things you witnessed will have made you strong
> enough to bear the power of my smile."
>
> (*Par.* 23.46–8)

The pilgrim's struggle to bear the weight of Beatrice's smile carries over into the Empyrean, where Dante reprises his entire relationship to his lady as a move from *riso* to *riso*. In *Paradiso* 30 he recalls what her salutation meant to him in the *Vita Nuova*, when everything depended on a smile granted or withheld. As it was in the beginning of his career, so now it is at its end: "the memory of her sweet smile / deprives me of the use of my own mind" (ll. 26–7). In the next canto, after Beatrice resumes her allotted place within the heavenly rose, Dante thanks her for her willingness to leave her footprints in Hell so as to liberate him for Heaven. She listens, "And she, / however far / away she seemed, smiled, and she looked at me. / Then she turned back to the eternal fountain" (31.91–3).

This retrospective might have brought up memories of his old unfaithfulness, but in Heaven we are beyond recrimination or regret. This point is made several times by the blessed when they make it clear that any backward glance toward a sinful life once lived or an intellectual error once committed no longer carries any reproach.[12] In the Heaven of Venus, for instance, the notorious Wife of Bath figure Cunizza confides that she long ago "indulged" or pardoned the erotic self-indulgence that characterized her worldly life – "and it does not grieve me" (*Par.* 9.35). Similarly, Folco of Marseilles, appearing in the same canto and sphere, confesses the imprint of Venus upon his former life; then he adds, "Yet one does not repent here; here one smiles – / not for the fault, which we do not recall, / but for the Power that fashioned and foresaw" (ll. 103–5). Likewise, when Gregory the Great arrives in Heaven, he sees the hierarchy of the angels and realizes that he "miscalculated" their ordering in his writings: "when Gregory came here – when he could see / with opened eyes – he smiled at his mistake" (28.134–5). What could be more liberating than a paradise in which a Pope called "the Great" is at ease with a mistake, can even find an error amusing?

The Empyrean marks the apotheosis of the smile. In fact, smiling is the signifier of the beatific vision, as Dante realizes when he takes in the whole of the City of God with a glance and notes that the blessed have faces "a carità süadi, / d'altrui lume fregiati e di suo riso," "given up to love – / graced with Another's light and their own smile ["di suo riso]," (31.49– 50). The fact that each of the blessed is adorned with his or her particular smile, suggests that each is unique. The smile turns out to be as person-specific as a fingerprint, or as the individualized seating within the hierarchy of the heavenly rose.

At the apex of the "candida rosa," the Blessed Virgin Mary brightens at the sight of more than a thousand "festive angels," each distinct in splendor and skill:

> And there I saw a loveliness that when
> it smiled at the angel's songs and games
> made glad the smiles of all the other saints.
>
> (*Par.* 31.133–5)

Mary's smile inspires a flash of recognition from the blessed. The loveliness ("bellezza") of her mouth as she rejoices in the angels' sublime play in turn calls forth "letizia" (gladness) in all their eyes. When Bernard offers his prayer to Mary – before she too, like Beatrice, looks upward to the eternal fountain of divine light – the Virgin's face expresses her joy at his words on behalf of the pilgrim: "The eyes that are revered and loved by God, / now fixed upon the supplicant, showed us / how welcome such devotions are to her" (33. 40–2). Once again her smile has a ripple effect, this time on Bernard, who in turn "was signing to me with a smile to look upward" (ll. 49–50). Yet "up" is a spiritual direction in which Dante is already moving, drawn as he is from the smiling faces of Mary and Bernard to the ultimate "face-to-face" vision of God.

As this detailed review of *riso* and *sorriso* should suggest, the smile is not only Dante's signature gesture but perhaps his most original and indeed useful contribution to medieval theology – or indeed to the Christian tradition itself, which has long found it easier to recall that "Jesus wept" (John 11: 35) than to imagine that he might have laughed as well. Despite the degree to which Dante is associated with the infernal, it is his creation of a "smile of the universe," radiant throughout Purgatory and Paradise, which shows his "spin" on the ancient religion he inherited. To be told that God the Trinity smiles upon himself; to see Gregory smiling at his former error; to catch the delight in Mary's eye that spreads like lightning throughout the heavenly rose; to consider that the resurrection of the body might mean the raising up of one's own distinctive smile; or to imagine seeing God "face to face" as an encounter with holiness that does not require eyes averted and lips closed tight, but rather entails the spontaneity of a smile returning a smile – to entertain any of these possibilities requires a "new life" for the Christian imagination that did not take place in Dante's fourteenth century and is now (sadly) long overdue.

In closing, one might say that the poet's faith, at least as we can discern it from his writing, was like that of most people – a mixture of received tradition and personal idiosyncrasy. He lived at a time of religious fervor but also of turmoil and crisis. Given his evangelical impulses, it was important for him to affirm the central teachings of Christianity: belief in the Triune God, the Incarnation of Christ, and the authority of the Scriptures, as well as the conversion of heart, soul, mind, and strength. At the same time, he made that orthodox faith very much his own. He took liberties when he wanted to, or when the dictates of his imagination "called" him to do so. Because his experience of Christ came to him most powerfully through the person of Mary and the figure of Beatrice, he affirmed the Incarnation in women's flesh. His poem became the "scripture" of his gospel, and over the course of the *Commedia* he so transfigured the human smile that it took on all the power of the sign of the cross. Whether inspired by the nine Muses or the Holy Spirit (or some Dantesque combination of the two), he gave us a new account of everything old.

Chapter 5

Dante's Afterlife

How to assess the enduring effect of a writer? To discover how thoroughly Shakespeare has permeated English-speaking culture one has only to realize the extent that a single play – say *Hamlet* – has entered our conversation: ''Frailty, thy name is woman!,'' ''to the manner born,'' ''more honour'd in the breach than the observance,'' ''neither a borrower nor a lender be,'' ''to thine own self be true'' all come from Act I alone. No Italian poet could hope for anything like this impact on our language. He might infiltrate our cultural imagination, however, as Dante in fact continues to do in the English-speaking world and in ways that show him to be a widely held cultural property.

Take the currency of the last line ''spoken'' by the gates of Hell: ''Lasciate ogne speranza, voi ch'entrate'' (*Inf.* 3.9). These words have become the stock in trade of *New Yorker* cartoonist Robert Mankoff, who knows that he can count on a least common denominator of recognition and a laugh: people can ''get'' Dante jokes without actually knowing the poet at all. In one cartoon captioned ''Vacation,'' for instance, he shows a crowded family station wagon heading toward a highway tunnel bearing the legend, "Abandon All Hope Ye Who Enter Here." In another he shows a troop of naked people entering an almost identical cavern whose superscript reads "Abandon All Hope, Ye Who Enter Here (If you have already abandoned all hope, please disregard this notice.)" Yet a third (see Figure 7) shows the same crowd advancing toward the inscription, "ABANDON HYPE, YE WHO ENTER HERE." The caption reads "P. R. Hell." Not to be outdone, cartoonist Edward Frascino gives us a composite scene from the *Inferno*: fire from heaven, a tangle of writhing sinners, a whip-wielding devil, and two laurel-crowned figures in the foreground. The cartoon reads: "Coming to a theatre near you – Dante & Virgil: A Buddy Movie" (see Figure 8).

Nor is Dante fodder for American cartoonists alone. Take what appeared on the front page of *The Independent* shortly after the 1997 passing of Britain's Protection from Harassment Act. In a take-off on the High Victorian painting by Henry Holiday, now in Liverpool's Walker Art Gallery, the lovelorn suitor of the *Vita Nuova* oversteps his legal bounds. "Tell that Dante Alighieri to bugger off," says one of Beatrice's companions, "or you'll do him for stalking."

Why make these connections with the author of the *Commedia*? Is Dante really necessary to make the point that family vacations are as hopeless as the eternal prospects of public relations agents? That the juxtaposition of poetry and computer-generated prose is amusing? That this summer's action adventure of a hero and his sidekick has a venerable prototype, which in turn becomes funny when you think of a classic as popular entertainment – which, as we've seen, the *Commedia* actually was in its own day?

It may be because of the poem's extraordinary visual potential that these humorists turn to Dante for their material. They also enjoy exploiting what happens when a classic rubs up

Figure 7 Robert Mankoff cartoon © The New Yorker Collection 1998 Robert Mankoff from cartoonbank.com. All Rights Reserved

against the banalities of contemporary life, the fun that comes of mixing the serious with the silly. Or maybe the appeal of the poem is more what we find in Edward Sorel's *New Yorker* cover, which not only capitalizes on the *Inferno* as a "how-to" guide for making eternal judgments but brings Dante up to date. On descending levels of damnation we find "Politicians who promised to cut taxes," then below them "Politicians who promised to balance the budget," and at the bottom of the heap, "Politicians who promised to cut taxes and balance the budget."

COMING *to a theatre near you—*

DANTE & VIRGIL
A BUDDY MOVIE

Figure 8   Edward Frascino cartoon © The New Yorker Collection 1991 Ed Frascino from cartoonbank.com. All Rights Reserved

The *Dante's Inferno Hell Test* comes immediately to mind when anyone is hungry for the thrill of eternal speculation. A feature of the Web (www.4degreez.com/misc/dante-inferno-test.mv), it offers the opportunity for self-diagnosis: ''Answer the questions below as honestly as you can and discover your fate. Based on your answers, your purity will be judged and you will be banished to the appropriate level of hell. Abandon all hope.'' Those insufficiently bad will be sent on their way to Purgatory, though without any sense of how much time will be spent on the various terraces. Anyone eager to think about other people can "Play Dante" on Columbia University's IL Tweb Digital Dante site. It offers the gamester wider options: just for fun, says the advertisement, you can "assign a person of your choice to heaven, purgatory, or hell." There is also a PlayStation game called "Devil May Cry", with a hero named Dante (half human/half demon), who has a twin brother, Virgil.

Popular allusions to Dante, if widespread, are not always accurate. Take the alleged quotation by "the great Italian poet" that currently comes up over 81,000 times on a Google search and turns out to be a pronouncement dear to the hearts of preachers, commencement speakers, and bloggers: "The hottest places in hell are reserved for those who in times of great moral crisis maintain their neutrality." This sentiment is certainly not foreign to "the great Italian poet," who refuses to name any of the neutrals precisely because he deemed their fence-sitting beneath contempt:

> The world will let no fame of theirs endure;
> both justice and compassion must disdain them;
> let us not talk of them, but look and pass.
>
> (*Inf.* 3.49–51)

Yet those who refused to take a moral position, and therefore who "were never alive," are *not* consigned "to the hottest places in hell": the poet is quite explicit that Inferno refuses them entry into its midst because to do so would be to give the rest of the damned a category of sinner to gloat over (3.40–2). Nor does fire burn at its "hottest" at the depth of Hell: the bottom of the universe, as we have seen, is ice cold. The spirit of the alleged quotation may very much be in keeping with the poet's attitudes toward fence-sitting, but it is literally false. Whoever made up the adage did not bother to read the *Commedia* very carefully.

A little Dante learning may not exactly be a dangerous thing, but it is far more common than real acquaintance. In fact, the poet is probably "known" more widely today by people who have never turned a page of the *Commedia* than by those who have. It is his *Inferno*, of course, that became the household word from the very outset. In our own time, Dante's depiction of evil is depravity's gold standard, the readiest way for journalists to suggest the unspeakable in the here and now. Terrible fires, egregious crimes, the worst atrocities all warrant the same comparison. "This is a tale of horrors," says a commentator on the intractable 10-year civil war in Sierra Leone, "[that moves] beyond the Gothic and into the realm of Dante's *Inferno*."[1]

Yet rather than suggesting only a nightmare, "Inferno" can also identify a night club, a bar and grill, an S&M boutique, indeed any commercial walk on the wild side. Not that Hell is Dante's sole legacy to us. The *Commedia* as a whole has been an inspiration for visual artists and composers, preachers and politicians, filmmakers and dramatists, and even for advertising copywriters. For instance, an Italian laxative marketed just after World War II was given the name "Beatrice" and its campaign built around a wildly misconstrued line, "I' son Beatrice che ti faccio andare" (*Inf.* 2.70) – "I am Beatrice who makes you go."[2] The name of Dante's beloved has currency and so was chosen to represent an unlikely product for the same reason that a rock group calls itself "The Divine Comedy." Everyone wants to be remembered, and banking on Dante's well-established reputation is one way to achieve that goal.

It is in the world of literature, however, that Dante has left his most indelible mark on culture. This is easy to understand in Italy, where his poetry helped forge a language – regional in the fifteenth century, national in the nineteenth – and where the *Commedia* remains a text studied in school and known by heart. Less predictable has been his impact on twentieth-century

Russian literature (Mandelstam, Akhmatova, Solzhenitsyn, Joseph Brodsky), on the Irish (Yeats, Joyce, Beckett, Seamus Heaney, Ciaran Carson) and even on contemporary Japanese fiction. Nobel Prizewinner Kenzaburo Oe's 1987 *Letters to My Sweet Bygone Years* describes a (failed) attempt to build a contemporary society around Dante's worldview. Another novel, *The Ruin of the Divine Comedy*, set at the time of a nuclear holocaust, has Dante serve as the novelist's guide through a tongue-in-cheek Inferno replete with prominent Japanese politicians, living and dead.

Dante in English

One could argue that the poet's most powerful presence outside of Italy has been in the English-speaking literary world, where his work has been (to quote Shelley's *Defense of Poetry*) "the bridge thrown over the stream of time, uniting the modern and the ancient world" (Shelley 1977, p. 498). This was first evident in the poetry of Geoffrey Chaucer (d. 1400), who knew Dante well enough to translate, imitate, and parody him in such poems as *The Parliament of Fowls*, and to such an extent that he could be described by a contemporary as "Daunt in Englysche" (*DEL*, 1, p. 19).[3] Yet the next 250 years mark a Dante oblivion, which ended only in the mid-seventeenth century with John Milton (d. 1674). Milton owned several of Dante's books (in Latin and Italian) and, together with other Protestants, found him to be an "Italian writer against the Pope" in the pages of his *Monarchia* and in the *Commedia*'s scathing denunciations of the papacy.[4] What was lost in this enthusiasm for pope bashing, of course, was the fact that Dante believed fervently in the See of Peter. He took issue not with the institution but with those who were corrupting it. Apart from whatever polemical use Milton made of Dante in his prose writings, *Paradise Lost* (1667) bears witness to an intermittent but ongoing dialogue with the *Commedia* through citation, allusion, and echo. Here is a "sacred poet" in seventeenth-century England, a writer with unmistakable biblical ambitions, who quite openly reveals his connection to the great "Reformer" of the Florentine Trecento.

Critical opinion turned against Dante (in England as on the Continent) in the Enlightenment, when neoclassical standards of decorum and a loathing of excess turned into overt hostility toward his work. In 1738 novelist, critic, and essayist Horace Walpole, showing all the prejudices of the Establishment, found the author of the *Commedia* "extravagant, absurd, disgusting, in short a Methodist parson in Bedlam" (*DEL* 1, p. 340). Twenty years later philosopher and polemicist Voltaire (d. 1778) was even more withering. He could understand why Dante might appeal to those with a taste for the bizarre, extravagant, and barbaric; the poet's reputation might even secure a place on some library shelves for his unbearable poem. But even if the *Commedia* was to be treasured for antiquarian reasons, it surely would never be *read*: who in his right mind would to do so? (*DEL*, 1, p. 207).

Such was Anna Seward's conviction as well. In 1805, this now-forgotten but once well-connected poet – celebrated as the "Swan of Lichfield" – held nothing back when she wrote to the Anglican clergyman Henry F. Cary about his translation of the *Commedia*. Despite Cary's good efforts on his behalf, Dante, to her mind, had produced "an epic poem consisting entirely of dialogue and everlasting egotism! Were you never struck by the presumptuous malice of design in this poem? With the inherent cruelty of the mind that could delight in suggesting pains and penalties at once so odious and so horrid?" Her indictment went on: "Dante is the only poet, of high reputation, whom I cannot understand" (*DEL*, 1, p. 403).

From Beyond the Pale to Cultural Centrality

Seward's take-no-prisoners attitude toward the author of the *Commedia* would soon seem incomprehensible. In fact, it was already dated when Seward wrote in 1805, for at the same time that she was venting her spleen over Dante's "transcending filthiness" (*DEL*, 1, p. 404), William Godwin acclaimed the poet as "one of those geniuses who in the whole series of human existence most baffle human calculation, and excite unbounded astonishment" (*DEL*, 1, pp. 641–2). A mere 50 years later, moreover, art historian and essayist John Ruskin celebrated Dante in *The Stones of Venice* (1851–3) as a universal cultural touchstone: he was "the central man in all the world"; in him one could find "the imaginative, moral, and intellectual faculties all at their highest" (Ruskin 1898, 3, p. 156).

Why this dramatic change of taste? It may have been inspired by the new German Romantic fascination with Dante that made its way from the Continent to England through Samuel Taylor Coleridge and others; or perhaps it was the enormous success of such paintings as Joshua Reynolds's 1773 "Count Ugolino and his Children in the Dungeon" or the Michelangelo-inspired drawings of Henry Fuseli meant to form a "Dante gallery" in London. Yet apart from a shift in Zeitgeist that opened people to what had been so recently deemed repellent, it was probably Henry F. Cary's appealing translation that gave so many English readers the opportunity to enjoy the poem for the first time.[5] Cary was not in fact the first to render the entire text into English: the Irishman Henry Boyd, another Anglican priest, took that honor in 1802. Nor was Cary's 1814 publication of *The Vision* – his title for the *Commedia* – an immediate success. Yet, only four years later, excellent appraisals in the *Edinburgh Review* by literary men with the clout of Coleridge and Ugo Foscolo turned Cary's Dante into a must-read. *The*

Vision went into multiple printings that made the poem available to a new generation that did not find the "Gothick" repellent; rather, they were drawn to it. In recognition of Cary's contribution to British letters he was given a place of honor in Westminster Abbey's Poet's Corner. It was he, in effect, who gave the nineteenth century "Daunt in Englysche." One can only imagine what Cary would have made of the fact that a current hip-hop rendition of the *Commedia* uses his (copyright free) version of the poem to sing the poet's song.

Among writers the Romantics were the first to succumb to Dante's allure.[6] William Blake made 98 colored drawings of the *Commedia* and was engraving scenes from the *Inferno* right up until his death in 1827. According to a biographer, he also held "visionary conversations" with Dante (along with Moses and the Hebrew prophets, Homer, and Milton): "All majestic shadows, grey but luminous, and superior to the common height of men" (*DEL*, 1, p. 456). John Keats took his copy of Cary with him in 1818, when he went hiking in Scotland and the Lake District. Percy Bysshe Shelley not only praised Dante to the skies in his *Defense of Poetry* but translated portions of the *Purgatorio* into English *terza rima*. In his last work, *The Triumph of Life*, he demonstrated how fully he had assimilated and transformed

> . . . the rhyme
> of him whom from the lowest depths of Hell
> Through every Paradise & through all glory
> Love led serene, & who returned to tell
> In words of hate & awe the wondrous story
> How all things are transfigured, except Love.
>
> (ll. 471–6)

Lord Byron showed the open influence of Dante both in *Childe Harold* (1818) and *Don Juan* (1819); like Shelley, he also tried his hand at *terza rima* translation (including a version of Paolo and Francesca's *Inferno* 5, which he called the ''Fanny of Rimini'' canto). In 1821 he published *The Prophecy of Dante* with the hope that someone would translate his poem into Italian so that it might reach its intended audience. Byron imagines the poet in a desolate Ravenna at the end of his life, surveying with trepidation what will befall his country-men in centuries to come. ''Unite'' in the face of foreign oppression, he tells them: their self-defense should be a common *national* cause. Conveniently forgetting the passion for world empire unambiguously proclaimed in the *Monarchia* and *Commedia*, Byron's Dante is at one with the Risorgimento struggle for Italian national independence from the Austro-Hungarian Empire and the papacy alike. At once an alienated ''Byronic'' hero on the fringes of his society and a poet standing in solidarity with all those seeking liberty, *The Prophecy*'s seer may have been scarred by his reversals of fortune but is unbowed by fate: ''Persecution, exile, the dread of a foreign grave, could not shake his principles'' (*DEL*, 2, p. 50).

Byron's particular notion of a melancholy prophet without honor in his own home soon took hold more generally. Dante became for many, as for Matthew Arnold, ''the grand, imprac-ticable Solitary'' (*DCH*, p. 612).[7] Thomas Macaulay wrote in 1825, ''There is perhaps no work in the world so deeply and uniformly sorrowful ... He was a man too sensitive and too proud to be happy'' (*DEL*, 2, p. 407). In Thomas Carlyle's 1840 lecture on the ''Hero as Poet,'' the *Commedia* is character-ized as ''the mournfulest of books''; it bears witness to ''the transcendent distemper of the noblest soul''; it is the ''utterance of a boundless, implacable sorrow and protest against the world'' (*DEL*, 2, p. 498). Robert Browning's lively dramatic monologues owe much to the self-revelations of Dante's characters, but for his wife, Elizabeth Barrett Browning, it was the poet's personal sadness that overwhelmed everything else about him. She could not think of "any man as poor / In mirth, to let a smile undo / His hard-shut lips" (*DEL*, 2, p. 462). Yet even before the suffering of exile made those lips "hard-shut," there was melancholy and sorrow aplenty. This portrait we also see in Dante Gabriel Rossetti's Pre-Raphaelite paintings of the young poet mid-swoon, as much in love with easeful death as with the diaphanous lady who refuses her salutation.

Nonetheless, mourning and melancholia were by no means the only way to imagine the poet: in the nineteenth century, Dante the man was considered to be as multifaceted as his work. Depending on the admirer, he was the harbinger of modern poetry, the liberator of vernacular speech, the civic leader, the wanderer and refugee, the prophet of nationalism, the advocate for a universal government, the exacting crafts-man, the master of the poetic monologue – a man for all seasons. To those struggling to liberate "Italy enslaved" (to recall the poet's lament in *Purgatorio* 6), he was the Founding Father of his country – a medieval Garibaldi.

As such he soon became required reading in Italian schools, and the *Commedia* a volume meant to adorn every home (rather like a Protestant's family Bible). A case in point: in 1890 Angelo De Gubernatis organized an "Esposizione Bea-trice" in Florence to honor "the glory of the Italian woman." Over 2,800 people came to the city to view thousands of exhibits and to attend Dante-related lectures, plays, and mu-sical performances. To promote the occasion, the ministry of education mandated that all Italian schoolchildren should write essays on the poet and his world.[8]

Meanwhile, across the sea in mid-nineteenth-century New England, Ralph Waldo Emerson took Dante as a model for a distinctly American genius.[9] Here was a man who could write autobiography "in colossal cipher" and whose eloquence was wide-ranging enough to be at home on the range: "Dante knew how to throw the weight of his body into each act," writes Emerson in a journal entry, "he knows 'God damn,' and can be rowdy if he pleases, and does please" (Emerson 1960, p. 342). At the urging of the Transcendentalist Margaret Fuller-Ossoli, who had married her way into Italian culture, Emerson made the first English-language translation of the *Vita Nuova* in 1843 – a manuscript lost in the depths of the Columbia University Library until roughly one hundred years later.

Dante's impact was even greater on one of Emerson's friends, Henry Wadsworth Longfellow. To deal with the sudden death of his beloved wife, he began to translate the *Commedia* at a time when he could not bring himself to do his own writing. Starting with the final canticle and translating over the course of three decades, he worked his way from the *Paradiso* back to the *Inferno*, finishing the entire project by 1865 – the six hundredth anniversary of the poet's birth. It was published three years later.

Longfellow was aided in his endeavor by a group of highly literate friends who called themselves the Cambridge Dante Club; they also established the Dante Society of America in 1881, several years before the Florentines organized a similar group in Italy. These New Englanders shared Longfellow's passion for Dante. With him they fought against Harvard's resistance to "modern languages" in general and all things Roman Catholic in particular. "Club" member James Russell Lowell translated the *Commedia* (into prose, perhaps to achieve a more literal rendering than was afforded by Longfellow's poetry), as well as the *Vita Nuova*. Their common intention was to bring Dante into New World circulation, to make him a local, even national sensation. Another member, Oliver Wendell Holmes, wrote in a sonnet addressed to Florence – the cruel city that had banished the one who should have been its favorite son – that Italy's loss had become America's great gain. His small group of fellow Cambridge poets, Holmes tells

Dante's birthplace, would happily "make thy dead immortal *ours*" (emphasis mine).

This appropriation did not mean that Dante was meant to be yet another European antiquity transported to the West, like those imported works of "fine art" shortly to be placed in Boston drawing rooms and museums. Rather, he would be an inspiration for the creation of a new and living culture, a genuinely American poetry. The study of Dante could help writers of all kinds discover a vernacular speech that was fresh, vibrant, and no longer subordinate to the English of the reigning monarch. President Theodore (Teddy) Roosevelt went as far in 1911 as to single out Dante's "art" and "soul" to point out what was missing in American letters. Nothing less would do justice to the true grit of the nation's life:

> The Bowery is one of the great highways of humanity, a high-way of varied interest, of fun, of work, of sordid and terrible tragedy; and it is haunted by demons, as horrible as any that stalk through the pages of the "Inferno." But no man of Dante's art and Dante's soul would write of it nowadays, and he would hardly be understood if he did. (Cited in Ahern 1989, p. 224).

Twentieth-Century Dante

Because a new century predictably turns against the tastes of its near ancestors, one would expect that the Dante beloved by Romantics, Victorians, and Pre-Raphaelites would rapidly fall out of favor with those after 1900 who were intent (in Ezra Pound's phrase) on "making it new." Quite the contrary: it was in the English-speaking twentieth century that Dante continued to be "altissimo poeta," the greatest of poets. The list of those who have been in ongoing conversation with him is both diverse and lengthy; it is also particularly rich in

Americans, whether by birth, acquired citizenship, or long-time residence. Ezra Pound and T. S. Eliot – American poets who made their way to England before World War I – come immediately to mind as Modernists who made Dante "modern." In the post-World War II generations that followed, there were first W. H. Auden, James Merrill, Robert Lowell, and then Derek Walcott, Charles Wright, Geoffrey Hill, W. S. Merwin, and Seamus Heaney.[10] One thinks as well of those now in their middle age such as Paul Muldoon (an Ulsterman living in Princeton) and Gjertrud Schnackenberg (in the United States). But this is only to name poets for whom Dante has been a preoccupation; there are many others who have made it a practice to visit his work occasionally but often to considerable effect (Czeslaw Milosz, Amy Clampitt, Louise Glück, Allen Grossman, Fred Chappell). And, of course, there are novelists who owe a more or less obvious debt: Joseph Conrad in *Heart of Darkness* (1902); James Joyce in both *Portrait of the Artist as a Young Man* (1916) and *Ulysses* (1922); C. S. Lewis in *The Great Divorce* (1945); Robert Penn Warren in *All The King's Men* (1946, with its epigraph from the *Purgatorio*); William Golding's *Free Fall* (1959); Amiri Baraka's *The System of Dante's Hell* (1965); Gloria Naylor's African-American Inferno in *Linden Hills* (1985); and most recently, Nick Tosches's *In the Hand of Dante: a Novel* (2002) and Matthew Pearl's immensely successful murder mystery, *The Dante Club* (2003).

Seamus Heaney

A more sustained look at one of the English-language writers fascinated with Dante may help to reveal the particular ways his poetic legacy has been taken on – in this case by a Nobel Prizewinner who combines in himself a Northern Irish upbringing, an appointment as Professor of Poetry at Oxford, and many years on the Harvard faculty. Seamus Heaney's engagement with Dante is most evident in three books of poetry spanning a little more than a decade: *Field Work* (1979), *Station Island* (1984), and *Seeing Things* (1991).[11] His brilliant translation of the Ugolino episode at the end of *Field Work* draws an implicit connection between the tragic political landscape of Northern Ireland and thirteenth-century Tuscany. Apparently his reading Dante in translation during the 1970s led him to recognize some of the conditions of Medieval Florence – the intensities, the factions, the personalities – as analogous to the Belfast situation. It was as if Dante had foreseen all the particularities of his local scene: "the combination of personality, political fury, psychological realism. All the voices speaking, and the accusations flying, the rage and the intimacy . . . '' (Heaney 1985, p. 18).

The volume *Station Island* takes its title from a sequence of 12 poems placed at the book's center. Heaney describes this work as connected series of "dream encounters" with ghosts, all set on Station Island on County Donegal's Lough Derg. His engagement with this traditional site of a penitential three-day vigil of fasting and prayer presents an occasion for self-confrontation and, finally, liberation. The ghosts the poet meets there represent significant elements of his past, both familial and intellectual; they are also a series of alter egos, versions of who he might have become under different circumstances. In this venture it was the *Commedia* that served as a model for what he was trying to achieve: "the local intensity, the vehemence and fondness attaching to individual shades, the ways personalities and values were emotionally soldered together, the strong strain of what has been called personal realism in the celebration of bonds of friendship and bonds of enmity" (Heaney 2003, p. 256).

Two of Heaney's old teachers appear, greeted with rueful affection, in an episode that recalls the pilgrim's meeting with his mentor Brunetto Latini in *Inferno* 15, as well as Eliot's famous reworking of this scene in the poet's encounter with a "familiar compound ghost" in *Little Gidding* (last of the *Four*

Quartets). Heaney also encounters William Carleton and Patrick Kavanaugh, Irish poets who themselves made the Lough Derg pilgrimage the subject of their verse. Heaney notes in his essay "Envies and Identifications" that Lough Derg was an overdetermined (and perhaps overworked) location, given the number of Irish writers (Sean O'Faolain and Denis Devlin as well as those named above) who had already written about it. Somehow, however, the intermediary of Dante's *Purgatorio* allowed this landscape of pilgrimage to become fresh territory.

Nonetheless, Heaney's ambivalence toward the traditional piety of Lough Derg, not to mention his Catholic upbringing, is dramatized in several *Station Island* encounters. In the first, Simon Sweeney, an "old Sabbath-breaker who has been dead for years" (Heaney 1985: 61), a "mystery man" from the poet's youth, warns him as he is about to begin the pilgrimage, "Stay clear of all processions" (p. 63). A priest he had known when a young man then asks him, "what are you doing here?," mindful that Heaney had long ago "gotten over" Catholic piety: "all this you were clear of you walked into / over again" (p. 70). In the last poem of the sequence, at the end of this extended sojourn with the dead, none other than the notoriously anticlerical James Joyce appears to cast aspersions on this "peasant pilgrimage" and to warn him off "any common rite" (p. 92).

Station Island is especially taken with violent, untimely deaths such as Dante assembles in Ante-Purgatory, the waiting place at the bottom of the mountain. In Heaney's case, the ghosts are all victims of Protestant–Catholic violence who force him to confront his own complicity and cowardice. Colum McCartney, the cousin for whom he had written an elegy in *Field Work*, shows up to indict the redemptive Dantesque transformation of his murder that Heaney had attempted previously in the *Field Work* poem, "The Strand at Lough Beg":

> You confused evasion and artistic tact.
> The Protestant who shot me through the head
> I accuse directly, but indirectly, you
> Who now atone perhaps upon this bed
> For the way you whitewashed ugliness and drew
> The lovely blinds of the *Purgatorio*
> And saccharined my death with morning dew.
>
>   (*Station Island*, VIII; Heaney 1985: 83)

Yet despite the poet's self-conscious regret, *Station Island* does not end in a spirit of remorse but rather with poems that suggest the "need and chance to salvage / everything" (p. 89). At the end, Heaney presents himself as a convalescent standing on the threshold of a new life. The sequence concludes with James Joyce boldly urging him to move on, to liberate himself from the political, religious, and even linguistic entanglements of his Irish past. Joyce charges him to swim out on his own, to "Let go, let fly, forget" (p. 93). The work concludes with a cleansing cloudburst that in effect brings the relief Heaney has been seeking all along. He is meant to give himself over, says Joyce, to "work lust" (p. 93).

Throughout *Station Island* the Dantesque oppositions between life and art, politics and literature, historical responsibility and private fulfillment surface through ghostly encounters. Heaney himself identified the core of the poem as a tension between contradictory allegiances. The claims of history, of the public and private past, of religion, on the one hand, are all given their due; yet Heaney grants himself permission to move beyond the impasse of these terms and oppositions. The ghosts rehearse the claims of the past with eloquent force, but then fade into silence. The poet can begin to write afresh.

The Artist's Dante

Dante's poem was from the beginning a magnet for artists and therefore for extensive visual interpretation – perhaps more powerful in its effect than any written commentary.[12] The manuscript illuminations of Giovanni di Paolo (d. 1483) for the *Paradiso* and the drawings of Sandro Botticelli (d. 1510) for the entire poem are works of exquisite craft; also remarkable are the handsome neoclassical engravings by John Flaxman (d. 1826) and the often gorgeous paintings and engravings by William Blake, both of which entered into the world of mass production as a result of the Dante craze that took off in England at the beginning of the nineteenth century. To this group of popularizers one must add Joshua Reynolds's painting of Ugolino and his sons, the wild Romanticism of Henry Fuseli (d. 1825), the dreamy visions of the *Vita Nuova* by Dante Gabriel Rossetti (d. 1882), and Gustave Doré's vivid interpretation of the whole poem (1861–68).[13] Nor was it only painters who took on the Dante poem. One thinks of Jean-Baptiste Carpeaux's sculpture of Ugolino and his sons (1865–67), now in New York's Metropolitan Museum, as well as of Rodin's monumental "Gates of Hell" (c. 1880–1917) in Paris.

Doré, who illustrated the Bible as well as such works as the *Thousand and One Nights* and *Don Quixote*, is at his very best in the *Inferno*. His engravings are theatrical, even operatic in their intensity; they were also made widely available through cheap reproduction and soon became how the poem "looked" for generations of readers. By the mid-twentieth century, however, this familiar vision was what serious artists needed to get out of their minds when they turned to Dante's text as inspiration for their own work. Amos Nattino, Salvador Dali, Leonard Baskin, Barry Moser, Robert Rauschenberg, Marcel Dzarma, Tom Phillips, and most recently Monika Beisner, have all tried their hand, often with beautiful results that are altogether different from one other. As can be seen in the cover design of this book, Beisner looks back lovingly to the fourteenth-century Sienese school of painting; Rauschenberg, on the other hand, is full of often amusing pop-culture references that open up new interpretive territory. In 2000 an illustrated *Commedia* ''for the new millennium'' appeared from Editions Nuages in Paris, with an *Inferno* by Lorenzo Mattotti, a *Purgatorio* by Milton Glaser (inventor of the ''I ♥ New York'' logo), and a Technicolor *Paradiso* by Moebius (aka Jean Giraud), who brings a paintbox to Doré's black and white. Most of these artists chose to be illustrators of the text and therefore stick quite close to its literal scene. Yet Tom Phillips, first in several *Commedia*-themed paintings and then at large in his striking, often witty *Inferno* (1983), offered a more personal and idiosyncratic visual commentary rather than what he calls the ''blow-by-blow illustrative description of the action.''[14]

The Commedia *in Performance: Drama, Film, Television*

The medieval illuminators who first turned their brushes to the *Commedia* brought to this vernacular newcomer the skills they had long demonstrated in the production of illustrated, lavishly decorated Bibles. With ancient technique brought to a very up-to-date text, the impressive appearance of the *Commedia* had a transformative effect on how it was first received. Commentary editions of the poem only reinforced the aura of *gravitas* surrounding it: here was a work in living Italian that was important, that was meant to be studied. Packaging helped make the poem a classic early on, at the same time that its popular diffusion and appeal kept it ''vulgar.''

The nascent Italian film industry in the early twentieth century took advantage of Dante as a crossover artist. Keen to

ennoble a new art form by making it part of the cultural establishment, they turned to the irreproachable *Commedia*, so recently revived during the independence movement as a
national treasure. Dante's presence in cinema, therefore, is as
old as the medium itself.[15] Between 1908 and 1912, as many as
11 (silent) films based on the poem were produced. Rather than
attempt the poem's big picture, directors typically presented
only selected scenes. These were the same old favorites that
had long attracted poets, painters, and sculptors – Paolo and
Francesca or Ugolino and his sons. The most influential of these
ventures was Milano Films' spectacular *Dante's Inferno* (1911):
it was lengthy, costly, and characterized by innovative special
effects that put it ahead of the competition. Divided into three
sections and 54 scenes, the film relied heavily on Gustave Doré
to provide a visual inspiration for each cinematic episode.

Hollywood followed suit in another decade or so. *Dante's
Inferno* (1924), promoted as ''A Spectacle of Drama and Beauty
Based on the Classic of Literature,'' also staged a succession of
episodes with the help of Doré's images, as Milano Films had
done not long before. A decade later Dante entered the world
of sound with *Dante's Inferno* (1935), a modern morality play
starring Spencer Tracy as a villain who owns a doomed
carnival horror house called (predictably enough) ''Dante's
Inferno.'' After its violent destruction, the man comes to himself in a dark wood of disaster: he is reborn just in time for
Hollywood's requisite happy ending.

Contemporary films that owe a debt to Dante are often more
oblique in their borrowing, though no less fundamental or
impressive for being so. This is especially evident in postwar
Italy, whether in Michelangelo Antonioni's *Red Desert* (1964)
or indeed in the lifetime work of both Pier Paolo Pasolini and
Federico Fellini. Several recent American movies – *Towering
Inferno* (1974), *Clerks* (1994), *Se7en* (1995), *Dante's Peak* (1997),
What Dreams May Come (1998), and *Hannibal* (2001) – also

make use of the *Commedia* and, in the case of *Se7en*, even feature a work of Dante criticism in the plot.

The measure and extent of genuine influence, however, is wildly varied. *Towering Inferno* concerns a high-rise fire and *Dante's Peak* an erupting volcano: both allude to the poem largely in order to evoke a sense of extreme horror. By contrast, *Clerks* give us a Dante–Virgil buddy movie as well as a chance to play irreverently with Catholic theology. *What Dreams May Come*, however, involves a larger Dantesque retelling (albeit one largely lost on the film's critics) that not only recalls the poem's preoccupation with the afterlife but specific episodes and themes from the *Commedia*, as well as Doré's engravings. A soul in bliss descends to Hell in order to rescue his lost beloved so that she can escape the wood of the suicides and see again the stars. The Beatrice figure in this case is played by none other than Robin Williams! Rather than the quality of casting choices, it is the movie's extraordinary special effects (and allusion to the rich tradition of Dante iconography) that prove most compelling.

Film has not been the only medium for Dante performance. In the beginning was the Lectura Dantis tradition begun by Boccaccio in Florence, whereby a scholar reads a canto and then comments on it. Such offerings continue to take place "live" in cities through the world; they also appear on Italian television, as in a program in the mid-1980s that made use of some of Italy's most prominent academic Dantisti serving as latter-day Boccaccios in the effort to bring the *Commedia* to the populace. Carrying on the tradition of marketplace entertainment (but at a level of sophistication and skill even Petrarch might have lauded), there have also been dramatic recitations of the poem by well-known actors such as Vittorio Gassman and Roberto Benigni

A truly spectacular staging of Dante was the dream of the American director Norman Bel Geddes. In 1921, after discovering the *Inferno* during a period of intense personal crisis, he resolved to establish a "Dante Theater" that would regularly produce the entire poem. Bel Geddes imagined a gigantic company of over 500 persons; he drew up plans for a production in New York's Madison Square Garden, as well as for various university auditoriums and open-air amphitheaters. His great hope was for a specially constructed theater in Chicago built for the sole purpose of bringing the *Commedia* to life on stage. This fantasy was never to come to pass, and yet it was at least partially realized in Italy decades later, between 1989 and 1991, when an avant-garde theatrical director engaged three major contemporary poets (Edoardo Sanguinetti, Mario Luzi, and Giovanni Giudici) to develop scripts for all three canticles. These were successfully produced in Prato and Bari.

Dante has not only been dramatized on the big screen and stage. In the late 1980s British filmmaker Peter Greenaway and artist-translator Tom Phillips collaborated on *A TV Dante*.[16] The series was daring, controversial, and not a little ridiculous (as when onscreen "commentary boxes" appear to provide the talking-head equivalent of footnotes). It was unable to garner sufficient interest or resources to advance beyond the first eight cantos of the *Inferno*. Nonetheless, *A TV Dante* explored how a relatively new medium might provide yet another vernacular for a "classic" text that was itself, of course, a medieval *volgarizzamento*, a translation of high into low.

Postmodern Dante

This same adaptation of old and new – this play with a venerable source in order to bring it "down" to our level and therefore to our attention – is evident in the work of Sandow Birk. Together with puppeteer Paul Zaloom, Birk in 2006 produced "Dante's Inferno, a Puppet Movie" that follows "the mullet-sporting Roman poet Virgil" and "our poet/puppet hero Dante" on a journey through our contemporary cultural wreckage: "past Homeland Security, sewage filled rivers, hellish hot tubs, grisly gated communities, and Satanic car dealerships" (http://www.dantefilm.com/dossier.html).

This movie grows out of the three-volume 2003–5 edition of the *Commedia* "translated" by Birk and Marcus Sanders into a California-inflected youth-speak that has been variously described by reviewers as "guy inarticulateness," "Valley girl," "laid back," "street slang," and "flat, vernacular, profane, irreverent stoner poetry." Purists of all kind are sure to be outraged; on the other hand, young people (along with anyone who prefers the vernacular to be vulgar) will have a good time. So too did an Italian couple I came upon in an American bookstore who, after being force-fed the "official" Dante in their *liceo* for the obligatory three years, were thrilled to discover *this* Dante. "Would it be translated into Italian?" they wondered.

Birk and Sanders speak of their work as an "adaptation"; I think of it as a paraphrase on the order of the 1960s *Cotton Patch* New Testament, or of Rob Lacey's even more contemporary *The Word on the Street*, which take liberties with another "sacred" text in order to make it accessible to people who would not otherwise pick up the Good Book. There's an "as told to" quality to this venture – or, better yet, a sense when reading it that someone has cornered you in a bar or a coffee shop with an unbelievable tale to tell. This kind of living language can have a very short shelf life, and it may well be that the frequently employed "whatever" in this text will go the way of "as if" from the 1990s, and therefore in no time appear embarrassingly out of touch. Nonetheless, the effect of their chattiness is to orient the entire poem in the direction of what critics have called Dante's "addresses to the reader," to generalize the urgent, immediate sense of those discrete moments in the *Commedia* when Dante speaks directly to the person turning his page in order to counsel, encourage, chide, or share a moment. Their overall tone is urban "Down Home."

When it comes to the artwork in this venture, Doré is everywhere recalled in Birk's carefully arranged poses, neoclassical allusions, and shadowy architectural settings. His work is in many ways as much about the French illustrator as the Italian poet. In this new *Inferno*, however, Doré's swirling Romanticism makes its way into the low life of a Los Angeles that is at once banal and menacing: strip malls, car dealerships, vandalized phone booths, back alleys, and highway over-passes. Birk's urban wasteland is populated by versions of Doré's contorted gymnasts, who less resemble ravaged sinners than the denizens of a gym gone haywire on steroids. It is an extraordinarily layered scene: Dante's damned souls as Doré imagined them, placed within an antiheroic City of Angels, and conjured by a postmodernist with a wicked sense of humor. As Birk moves through the poem, Los Angeles morphs into other urban scenes: *Purgatorio* settles in San Francisco and *Paradiso* makes its home primarily in New York.

The great tradition of Dante illustration usually transported the poem out of our world and presented it as an alternative universe unto itself. Birk, however, takes his clue from the poet who made his *Inferno* relevant to contemporary readers by referring them to people and places they already knew – notorious women and infamous men, a Roman bridge, a Sien-ese fountain, a Bolognese tower, a plunging waterfall that quite specifically "reverberates above San Benedetto / del-l'Alpe as it cascades in one leap" (*Inf.* 16.100–1). Birk's Hell comes to us via the sleazy parts of a postindustrial America which, like Dante's Inferno, is relentlessly urban and often decayed. Yet in this city of the damned, all is not in fact lost; nor does Birk fail to cherish the urban wasteland, warts and all. His portrayal is also funny, full of anachronisms and wacky allusions to popular culture. For instance, a two-storey inflated Fred Flintstone, flanking an escalator in a Los Angeles megastore, is the artist's version of the giant (Antaeus) who deposits Virgil and Dante in Hell's lowest circle (see Figure 9).

But precisely because of the sustained jocularity, much of the substance of Dante's poem vanishes, especially in *Purgatorio* and *Paradiso*. Irony is the natural element for Birk and Sanders, and therefore they are home free in the *Inferno,* where their exuberant spin on Los Angeles corresponds to Dante's own bittersweet (bordering on savage) relationship to Florence. Hell is a hall of funhouse mirrors, and nobody is supposed to look good for long. In this *Commedia* we can feel the spirit of James Joyce's *Finnegan's Wake* and its joshing of "the divine comic Denti Alligator"; or of Samuel Beckett in the 1930s, who told a friend, "All I want to do is sit on my ass and fart and think of Dante."[17] *Purgatorio* and *Paradiso,* however, present major problems for the ironist. So much in these canticles asks to be taken straight, seen as beautiful and good, even sublime. Dante's Heaven may be full of smiles, but it is smirk-free.

Doré attempted to capture the *Paradiso*'s Empyrean through dense swirls of indistinct angels, ten thousand times ten thousand revolving around a central luminosity – an empty space, perhaps corresponding to the divine excess that the poet cannot finally articulate. In this image he was considerably more successful than elsewhere in his *Paradiso*, whose illustrations have none of the energy and invention of his *Inferno* and largely dissolve into the pious cliché of his times: a plaster saint Beatrice, a surfeit of diaphanous robes and angel wings. Birk will have none of this. His vision of the cross that Dante glimpses when he ascends to the Heaven of Mars (*Par.* 14) is not Doré's crucifix held aloft by a swarm of angels; it is, rather, the sun setting through the crossed supports of the Williamsburg Bridge, seen by Dante and Beatrice from a

Figure 9 Sandow Birk, ''Antaeus''
Sandow Birk *Dante's Inferno - Canto XXXI: The Descent to the last Circle*, 2003.
Ink on Mylar 17"×14". Courtesy of the artist and Catharine Clark Gallery,
San Francisco, CA

trash-strewn vacant lot. Paradise is now, as close as Brooklyn and the Lower East Side.

Most surprising of all, however, is Birk's rendering of the City of God. For the realm of the imageless ineffable at the end of the *Paradiso*, Dante constructs a metaphoric impossibility that can be "seen" only by switching back and forth between the white rose (flower of both Venus and Mary) and a coliseum structure that is at once the New Jerusalem and a New Rome. Birk's sense of an ending borrows Doré's view of the Empyrean as a swirl of circles around an apparently empty vortex (see Figure 10). But in perhaps his most remarkable rethinking of his sources – of Dante's poem as well as of Doré's

Figure 10   Gustave Doré, "Empyrean"
The Doré Illustrations for Dante's Divine Comedy / Gustave Doré / Dover Publications

engravings – the still-point of the Empyrean's turning world becomes the Kaabah at the heart of Mecca (see Figure 11). We have all seen the photographs: a vast number of the white-robed devout circle the shrine at the center of a plaza, within which lies a sacred black stone said to have been given to Abraham by the archangel Gabriel. This holiest of objects draws the faithful from all over the world. They direct their prayers toward it five times a day wherever they may be, and make Mecca the destination of an obligatory once-in-a-lifetime pilgrimage.

The cultural appropriation is breathtaking. An Islamic City of God Paradise is envisioned for a poet who savaged Mohammed in *Inferno* 27, and went on to lambaste contemporary popes for failing to mount a Holy Land crusade. Birk is having fun with every kind of religious absolutism and exclusivity: "Wouldn't that be a twist if when the catholics get to heaven, it's a muslim place?" (email, 8/16/2004). And yet despite his tweaking of theological hardliners of all persuasions, his choice of the Kaabah and its devotees as the location of holiness is meant to be taken seriously: "I would like to imagine a heaven where everyone can go – the Jews, the Muslims, even 'the people from near the Ganges' who have never heard of Jesus" (email, 8/30/04). In this twenty-first-century makeover, *Paradiso* is made to look beyond its own boundaries. Dante becomes multicultural far and away beyond his own wildest dreams.

Commedia *in Comics*

Sandow Birk owes something to comic strip art in his "vulgarization" of Dante, but it is in the work of Gary Panter that cartoon becomes the artist's stock in trade. "Jimbo" is his errant pilgrim and "Valise" – a robot parole officer – his guide. In the *Inferno* installment of what is on the way to becoming a trilogy,

Figure 11 Sandow Birk *Dante's Paradiso - Canto XXXI: The Rose of Heaven*, 2005. Ink on Mylar 17"×14". Courtesy of the artist and Catharine Clark Gallery, San Francisco, CA

this post-punk Dante and Virgil make their way through the kitschy world of an immense shopping mall. Each step they take, each page of the work, is based on a specific canto. *Jimbo in Purgatory* continues the tale, once again canto by canto, with Dante's dramatis personae of thirteenth-century Italians taken over by faded TV stars, toys, robots, and pop ''icons.'' Just as Dante encounters musicians and poets along his way up the mountain, so Jimbo and Valise meet the likes of Tiny Tim, Boy George, and John Lennon. The angel who represents gentleness on the Terrace of Wrath is a teddy bear. Mythological figures, who came to Dante most often from Ovid, now metamorphose into a menagerie of Disney creatures. And the ferocious guardian of Purgatory, Cato, turns into Kung-fu megastar Bruce Lee (perhaps largely on the basis of his role as ''Kato'' on the TV show, ''The Green Hornet'').

According to Panter's Introduction, Purgatory is a ''vast testing center and all the participants strive for University degrees in literature. Each must respond with a literary fragment, a quotation that demonstrates knowledge of the passage and an ability to quote other works alluding to the theme of that location in the poem'' (Panter, 2005). The first-time reader of this book might be forgiven for taking it as a parody. It seems like a Dante-themed ''Trivial Pursuit'' intended for retentive comparative literature majors as well as for aficionados of game shows – people who have the required trigger-quick powers of recall but not necessarily any depth of understanding. The density of reference is well-nigh impenetrable. This ''testing center'' seems designed to flunk every contestant, its ''University in literature'' reserved for Panter alone.

Much is demanded of the would-be degree-seeker: not only knowledge of Dante and his medieval tale-spinning descendents (such as Boccaccio in his *Decameron* and Chaucer in the *Canterbury Tales*), but also a familiarity with Botticelli's illustrations of the *Commedia*, which serve Panter as Doré does Sandow Birk. In addition to these cultural high-water marks, moreover, Panter requires a total recall of pop lyrics, TV reruns, and the whole throwaway celebrity culture of the last few decades. This is truly catholic "infotainment."

The journey up the mountain takes Jimbo from a Hell's Mouth, based on medieval art, and culminates in a suburban Eden in which ancient and modern are jumbled together. Matelda is dressed in the skimpy attire of a Dallas Cowboys cheerleader (see Figure 12). She sports the regulation hat and boots, and wears a pleated micro-skirt that barely covers her buttocks (which are exposed, in gold, on the book's richly embossed cover). Every step of the way, Jimbo must crack a code, solve a puzzle, receive a password.

Figure 12   Gary Panter, *Jimbo in Purgatory*
Copyright © 2004 Gary Panter, published by Fantagraphics Books

But to what end? Perhaps the goal is to teach us how to connect the dots of a fragmented culture in which high and low, ancient and postmodern, serious and silly are all confounded? ''These fragments I have shored up against my ruin,'' says one of the voices that rise up despairingly from Eliot's *The Waste Land*. Yet Panter will have no Modernist gloom about the center no longer holding. The overall mood of his cartoon *libello* is celebratory – it is a comic book after all, despite the imposing 14'' by 24'' size, luxurious hardcover format, and quasi-scholarly apparatus.

The full title of Panter's work is *Jimbo in Purgatory: Being A Misreading of Dante Alighieri's Divine Comedy in Pictures and Unnumbered Footnotes*. Perhaps, as with Birk and Sanders, the only way to read the monumental past is to *mis*read it, to let the goofiness of the comic book figures and their balloon text messages have their say – ''HOW MUCH LONGER NOW FERSHITSAKES?'' asks the impatient Valise/Virgil in a slow moment on one of the terraces – and then see what is left in the end. Panter takes a distinct pleasure in ruins, emits a sense of excitement that comes from rummaging about in cultural trash where there is always the prospect of treasure to be found. No matter that there may be nothing to figure out at the end of his purgatorial quiz show, no change of mind and heart such as Dante brings about in his pilgrim. Perhaps what we have is a celebration of answers themselves – ''Trivial Pursuit,'' in fact – without the need for any overriding question, and certainly not those eternal ones that are ultimately a matter of life and death. Maybe the important thing to do with Dante is simply to *play*.

What Next?

Shelley presented Dante as a time bomb that continues at intervals to detonate. In his *Defense of Poetry*, written early in

England's nineteenth-century Dante craze, he likened the poet's individual words to sparks: each is "a burning atom," each "pregnant with lightning" (Shelley 1977: 500). All that awaits an explosion into poetry is a suitable conductor, a present-day lightning rod able to bring the *Commedia*'s power into new birth. In the early 1930s, Mandelstam alters this metaphor but maintains its implication. The poem is an engine that won't stop – a powerhouse, a flow of current. His Dante is a rocket always ready to be launched anew: "It is unthinkable to read the cantos of Dante without aiming them in the direction of the present day. They were made for that. They are missiles for capturing the future" (*PD*, p. 67).

The missile is prevented from striking its next target, according to Mandelstam, because of the *Commedia*'s status as an established, and therefore Establishment, text. The poem has been held fast in the grip of schoolroom rhetoric, bled dry by "the work of generations of scholastics, creeping philologists and pseudo-biographers" (*PD*, p. 90). It needs to be set free from their deadly grip. But what would this liberation of the text look like? Mandelstam gives us a scenario that is worthy of the audacious author of the *Paradiso*. In fact, he offers one of the self-consuming similes that makes Dante's final canticle such an extended tour de force:

> If the halls of the Hermitage were suddenly to go mad, if the paintings of all the schools and great masters were suddenly to break loose from their nails, and merge with one another, intermingle and fill the air in all the rooms with a Futurist roar and an agitated frenzy of color, we would then have something resembling Dante's *Commedia*. (*PD*, p. 90)

Imagine reader – as Dante often says – a world-class museum gone berserk. Imagine "period rooms" forgetting their timelines, and discrete canvasses "of all the schools and great masters'' flocking together like birds on the wing or like streams joining in a single torrent. Sight becomes sound as paintings ''roar,'' and the ancient and venerable turns Futurist and frenzied. Imagine a museum in meltdown and then you would have only ''something'' like, a mere resemblance of, Dante's poem.

It may be that Sandow Birk and Gary Panter, for all that they may lack in rendering the big picture, or of reading Dante ''aright,'' have captured the spirit of Mandelstam's fantasy better than the professional keepers of the flame. They have also, in their way of exuberantly taking liberties with their sources, been like the poet himself – who never scrupled to make use of other writers without particular regard for the integrity of their work, just as he rewrote (and in that sense misread) when it suited him.

Lacking in the work of Birk and Panter, to be sure, is the sense of grandeur and high purpose that keeps many returning to the poem for more than literary pleasure. ''Dante remains the great Buddhistic center of absolute attention and regard,'' writes the American poet Charles Wright, ''the true magnetic field of seriousness toward which all poems gravitate'' (*PD*, p. 262). Nor do the ironists catch the moral and political urgency that propels the *Commedia* from its first canto to its last. For this sensitivity one has to turn (at least in our time) to Russians like the exiled and imprisoned Mandelstam, who understood how Dante's conversations with the damned are ''conducted with that intense passion reserved for the prison visit'' (*PD*, p. 63); who saw that in fourteenth-century Italy, as in his own Stalinist world, ''Nightmares of prison life were imbibed like mother's milk'' (*PD*, p. 76).

A similar sensitivity is to be found among contemporary poets of Northern Ireland, like Seamus Heaney and Ciaran Carson, who have found in the internecine warfare of Florence a foreshadowing of their Troubles. When translating

Dante's description of Malebolgia in *Inf*. 18, Carson was reminded of his own Belfast:

"Rings of ditches, moats, trenches, fosses / military barriers on every side": I see a map of North Belfast, its no-go zones and tattered flags, the blackened side-streets, cul-de-sacs and bits of wasteland stitched together by dividing walls and fences. For all the blank abandoned spaces it feels claustrophobic, cramped and medieval. Not as beautiful as Florence, perhaps, but then Florence is "the most damned of Italian cities, wherein there is place neither to sit, stand, or walk," according to Ezra Pound. And we see again the vendetta-stricken courtyards and surveillance towers of Dante's birthplace, where everyone is watching everyone, and there is little room for manoeuver." (Carson 2002, pp. xi-xii)

In addition to the one-off marvel of Dante's individual genius, which remains a miracle no matter how you evaluate his work, perhaps in the end it takes a global village of artists and writers to make a *Commedia* – or at least a hive full of bees "endowed with the brilliant stereometric instinct," as Mandelstam would have it (*PD*, p. 55). It may take time and good luck for lightning to strike or the missile to fire. Or maybe the old magic will not happen the same way again, so that the task of new generations will be to take from the Dante hive whatever they can and make of its richness whatever they want. The *Commedia* has helped centuries of people to see the personal in the collective and universal, to find patterns of significance in the chaos of experience, and the grace of a smile in the tears of things. Weighty with the past, Dante has always been making it new. There is no reason to doubt he will continue to do so.

Notes

Prologue

1 Annotated, bilingual, paperback editions of the *Commedia* are plentiful. See for instance the three-volume translations of John D. Sinclair, John Ciardi, Thomas Bergin, Charles S. Singleton, Mark Musa, and Allen Mandelbaum. Robert Durling has produced impressively annotated editions of *Inferno* and *Purgatorio*, with a *Paradiso* volume on the way. So too have Robert and Jean Hollander. Although there are stylistic problems with Dorothy L. Sayers' rhyming translation of the entire poem, her notes are inspired. The text I refer to here is Allen Mandelbaum's.

Chapter 1 Dante's Life and Works

1 For a study of Domenico's painting see Altrocchi (1931).
2 To learn what the fourteenth century made of the poet, see *The Earliest Lives of Dante* and Salvadori (*DM*, pp. 43–69). For the next century's view, see Gilson (2005); see also Giuseppe Mazzotta, "Life of Dante," *CCD*, pp. 1–13, and "Alighieri, Dante," *DE*, pp. 15–20. Short, book-length "lives" are

offered by Barbi (1954), Bemrose (2000), Holmes (1980), Lewis (2001), and Hollander (2001); for the particular importance of Florence in Dante's work, see Lewis (1995) and Keen (2003). In my opinion the most useful presentation of Dante's life and works is by William Anderson (1982), to whom I am greatly indebted in this chapter.

3   For what Dante's military service may have consisted of, see Meek (1995, pp. 15–17).

4   John Najemy gives a lucid account of the intricacies of Florentine politics in Dante's day both in "Dante and Florence," *CCD*, pp. 80–99, and "Florence," *DE*, pp. 386–403. Behind the conflict between the Guelph parties stands an earlier division between Ghibellines and Guelphs that bedeviled life in the city for the generation before Dante's own. Annotated versions of the *Commedia* help unravel the political thicket with footnotes that clarify this or that character's affiliations. The "back story" is presented most lucidly in Anderson (1982, pp. 53–67), Lewis (2001, pp. 62–84), Meek (1995), and Waley (1988, pp. 145–56).

5   On exile in medieval Italy, the fullest coverage is given by Starn (1982), esp. "Dante and his Judges," pp. 60–85; see also Meek (1995, pp. 19–26).

6   For the significance of Henry VII of Luxembourg, see Anderson (1982, pp. 210–14) and Meek (1995, pp. 26–8).

7   Davis (1984, pp. 137–65), gives a very readable account of education in Florence that suggests what would have been available to someone like Dante.

8   See Petrucci (1995), "Reading and Writing Volgare in Medieval Italy," pp. 169–235.

9   See Anderson (1982, pp. 224–5).

10   All citations of the Bible are from the Latin Vulgate as translated in the Douay-Rheims version (1610).

11   Leo (1951, p. 60). See also Curtius (1963, p. 358):

The conception of the *Commedia* is based upon a spiritual meeting with Virgil. In the realm of European literature there is little which can be compared with this phenomenon. The "awakening" of Aristotle in the thirteenth century was the work of generations and took place in the cool light of intellectual research. The awakening of Virgil by Dante is an arc of flame which leaps from one great soul to another.

12 Cited by Corinna Salvadori in "Landmarks in the Fortunes of Dante in the Florentine Quattrocento," *DM*, p. 54.
13 On what Dante's library may have consisted, as well as on his overall access to books, see Petrucci (1995, pp. 212–13).
14 Ahern (1997) gives an excellent succinct account of how the *Commedia* was produced, received, and performed. See also his "Binding the Book" (1982).
15 Ahern (2003, p. 12).
16 See Ahern (1982, esp. pp. 800–1), and Gabriella Pomaro (*DE*, pp. 198–201) on the manuscript tradition.
17 For the *Commedia*'s probable audience, see Ahern (1997, esp. pp. 217–18, and 2003, pp. 8–9), Petrucci (1995), "Reading and Writing Volgare in Medieval Italy," pp. 169–235, and Gillerman (1988) on the illustrated manuscript evidence.

Chapter 2 Dante's Journey to God

1 Alison Morgan (1990) gives an excellent overview of the visionary sources and lore Dante drew upon in his construction of the *Commedia* in *Dante and the Medieval Other World*.
2 Le Goff (1986) tells the story of the "invention of Purgatory" in the Middle Ages and Dante's particular role as its most articulate interpreter.
3 The Church taught that Christ's personal resurrection three days after his death would be followed by a general resurrection of all the dead at the end of time. Christ would return, as the Creed says, "to judge the quick [i.e., living] and the dead." At this point, the souls in Purgatory would complete their penance. Because it was unimaginable to separate the soul from the body in eternity, the General Resurrection of the Dead would mean that both the damned

and the blessed would have some semblance of their bodies restored to them. This reuniting of the self would mean an increased sense of loss and suffering for the damned and of beatitude for the saints. Dante deals with these issues in *Inferno* 13, *Purgatorio* 25, and *Paradiso* 14.

4   For the fuller story of Virgil's prominence in Christian culture, see Comparetti (1997).

5   For the literature of vision and apocalypse, written both in Latin and the vernacular, see Gardiner's helpful collection of texts, *Visions of Heaven & Hell Before Dante* (1989).

6   Teodolinda Barolini (1993) argues otherwise.

7   The term "Limbo" refers properly to (1) the temporary place or state of the ancient souls of the Old Testament just, who, faithfully awaiting the Messiah, were excluded from the beatific vision until Christ's triumphant ascension into Heaven; or (2) the permanent place or state of those unbaptized children who, dying without grievous personal sin, are excluded from the beatific vision on account of original sin alone (the *limbus infantium* or *puerorum*). See the entry "Limbo" in *The Catholic Encyclopedia* (New York: The Encyclopedia Press, 1913, vol. 9, pp. 256–9). Dante includes the infants in his presentation and refers to the rescue of the ancient Hebrews after Christ's descent to the dead. His attention is fixed, however, on Limbo-dwellers the Church never imagined to be there: virtuous pagans (such as Virgil, Aristotle, and Plato) who lacked baptism but were otherwise without fault – a theological impossibility for an adult! See Virgil's discussion of his spiritual plight in *Purg.* 3.23–45 and 7.28–36. The salvation of infants is discussed in *Par.* 32. 40–84. For a discussion of Dante's handling of Limbo, see Hawkins (1999, pp. 99–124) and Iannucci (1979–80).

Chapter 3 Dante's Beatrice

1   Joan Ferrante offers an excellent discussion of Beatrice in *DE*, pp. 89–95, as well as in "Dante's Beatrice" (1992). See also Williams (1961) and Singleton (1958b).

2   Valency (1958) ends his study of medieval love poetry with
    a chapter (pp. 256–72) that shows Dante's debt to his pre-
    cursors as well as suggesting the "new life" he brought to
    the vernacular amatory tradition.
3   Martha Nussbaum puts it this way:

[The] final position of the poem is that any love is better the closer it is
to chastity (procreation in marriage always excepted). But this means
that if there is any depth of passion that demands sex for its full expression, or any knowledge of particularity and agency that seems to be
completed only by sexual agency, or, indeed, any poetry that seems to
be "dictated" by the body's love and expressive of its joy – these would
have to be omitted from the ascent.   (Nussbaum 2001, p. 585)

    Without reference to Nussbaum, Psaki (2000 and 2003)
    argues against this notion; Pertile (2003) endorses it whole-
    heartedly.
4   Williams also had an enormous impact on Dorothy L.
    Sayers's understanding of the poet, as is clear from her
    two volumes of lectures on Dante as well as in the notes
    that accompany her Penguin translation of the *Commedia*.
    See Reynolds (1989).
5   This story is told by Hadfield (1983, pp. 55–88). See also
    Shideler (1966).
6   The unlikelihood of the Vision of Eros surviving cohabit-
    ation, for instance, did not preclude the possibility for
    Auden:

This does not mean that one must under no circumstances marry the
person whose glory has been revealed to one, but the risk of doing so is
proportionate to the intensity of the vision. It is difficult to live day after
day, year after year, with an ordinary human being, neither much better
or much worse than oneself, after one has seen her or him transfigured,
without feeling the fading of the vision is the other's fault.   (*PD*, p. 137)

7   For the context of the letter in Auden's life, as well as the
    text itself, see Dorothy Farnan, *Auden in Love* (New York:

Simon and Schuster, 1984), pp. 65–6. The letter is in the Auden collection at the University of Texas at Austin, Humanities Research Center.

Chapter 4 Dante's Religion

1   For Dante's likely experience in the "schools of the religious," see Davis (1984, pp. 137–65).
2   These characterizations of lively address are from *De eruditione praedicatorum*, a thirteenth-century Dominican preacher's manual; cited by Carlo Delcorno, *Giordano da Pisa e l'antica predicazione volgare* (Florence: Olschki, 1975), 31.
3   Lesnick (1989, pp. 93–5) contrasts the two styles of Mendicant preaching, as well as the social and class biases of each order.
4   For lay religious life in medieval Florence, see Swanson (1995, pp. 102–35) and Vauchez (1993, pp. 107–17).
5   Henry of Susa, cited by Vauchez (1993, p. 113).
6   Jorge Luis Borges would agree: "There is a character missing in the *Commedia*, one who could not be there because he had become too human. That character is Jesus. He does not appear in the *Commedia* as he appears in the Gospels; the Jesus of the Gospels could not be the Second Person of the Trinity that the *Commedia* requires" (*PD*, p. 130).
7   Of the apocryphal Marian tales Dante gives only St Anne, the Virgin's mother, who is not mentioned in Scripture, but nonetheless takes her place within the City of God: "Facing Peter, / Anna is seated, so content to see her daughter / that, singing hosannas, she does not move her eyes" (*Par.* 32.132–c5).
8   *Bonaventure: the Soul's Journey to God, the Tree of Life, The Life of St. Francis*. The Classics of Western Spirituality, trans. Ewert Cousins (London: SPCK, 1978).
9   Meister Eckhart, *Meister Eckhart: A Modern Translation*, trans. Raymond Bernard Blakney (New York: Harper, 1941), p. 245.

10 Friedrich Nietzsche, "Skirmishes of an Untimely Man" 1, in *Twilight of the Idols* (1895).

11 James Knowlson, *Damned to Fame: The Life of Samuel Beckett* (London: Bloomsbury, 1996), p. 279, n. 31. My thanks to Professor Christopher Ricks for making this connection.

12 See Rachel Jacoff, "The Post-Palinodic Smile: Paradiso VIII and IX," *Dante Studies*, XCVIII (1980), pp. 111–22.

Chapter 5 Dante's Afterlife

1 *San Francisco Chronicle*, 7/5/2004, A: 5.

2 Iannucci (2004b), p. 3.

3 Wallace (1993) gives an excellent overview of Dante in English, beginning with Chaucer and moving to the present day. Too late for me to make use of is Griffiths and Reynolds, *Dante in English* (2005) with its anthology of "encounters between Dante and English-speakers across more than six centuries."

4 For Dante and Reformation England, see Havely (2003).

5 See Braida (2004) on the visual reception of Dante in the eighteenth century (pp. 9–26) and on the significance of Cary's translation (pp. 27–55).

6 For the English Romantics and Dante, see Ellis (1983); on Shelley and Byron, Pite (1994); and relevant essays in Havely (1998) on Gray, Blake, and Shelley.

7 For the Victorians and Dante, see Ellis (1983); on Robert Browning and Dante Gabriel Rossetti, Milbank (1998).

8 For the National Woman's Exposition centered on Dante's Beatrice, see De Gubernatis (1900, pp. 470–94). I am grateful to Professor Peter Rietbergen for the reference.

9 For Dante in nineteenth-century America, see La Piana (1948) and Pearl (1999).

10 For Dante and twentieth-century poets, see Ellis (1983) on Yeats, Pound, and Eliot; McDougal (1985) on Yeats, Pound, Eliot, Auden, Wallace Stevens, Samuel Beckett, and Laurence Binyon; and Havely (1998) on Pound, MacNeice,

Beckett, Gloria Naylor, Derek Walcott, and Seamus Heaney. See also Hawkins and Jacoff (2001), *The Poets' Dante*.

11   For a fuller study of Heaney and Dante, in conjunction with T. S. Eliot, Derek Walcott, Charles Wright, and Gjertrud Schnackenberg, see Hawkins and Jacoff (2003).

12   For the illuminated manuscripts of the *Commedia*, see Brieger, Meiss, and Singleton (1969). The five volumes of the *Enciclopedia dantesca* have beautiful full-color plates of art related to the *Commedia*; there is also lavish illustration in Taylor and Finley (1997), *Images of the Journey*.

13   See John W. Pope-Hennessey, *The Illustrations to Dante's "Divine Comedy" by Giovanni di Paolo* (New York: Random House, 1993); Hein-Thomas Schultze Altcappenberg, *Sandro Botticelli: The Drawings for the "Divine Comedy"* (London: Royal Academy of Arts, New York: H. H. Abrams, 2000); Corrado Gizzi (ed.), *Flaxman e Dante* (Milan: Gabriele Mazzotta, 1986); Milton Klonsky, *Blake's Dante: The Complete Illustrations to the "Divine Comedy"* (London: Sidgwick & Jackson, 1980); Corrado Gizzi (ed.), *Füssli e Dante* (Milan: Gabriele Mazzotta, 1985); Corrado Gizzi (ed.), *Dante Gabriel Rossetti e Dante* (Milan: Gabriele Mazzotta, 1984); Gustave Doré, *The Illustrations for Dante's 'Divine Comedy': 136 Plates* (New York: Dover, 1976).

14   In his work on the *Inferno* Phillips decided to avoid straightforward illustration of the text in favor of images that were "more analytic and exegetic": "This decision was prompted by the study of previous illustrated versions which so often seem to depict exactly those things that Dante himself describes most pictorially; they render a suggested infinite in finite terms and substitute certainties for the resonant ambiguities of the poem" (Phillips 1992, p. 237).

15   See the essays in Iannucci (2004a) as well as his entries in the *DE* on "Dante and Film" (pp. 246–50) and "Dante and Television" (pp. 283–6).

16   For analyses of "A TV Dante" see Vickers (1995) and Taylor (2004).

17   Cited by Hugh Haughton, "Purgatory Regained? Dante and Late Beckett," in Havely (1998), p. 142. In an unpublished poem Dante is characterized by Beckett as a "screechy flat-footed Tuscany peacock" that "stinks eternal" (pp. 141–2). For the fullest account of Dantean allusions in Beckett's poetry, see Lawrence E. Harvey, *Samuel Beckett, Poet and Critic* (London: Thames & Hudson, 1970).

Bibliography

Ahern, John (1982). "Binding the Book: Hermeneutics and Manuscript Production in *Paradiso* 33." *PMLA* 97, pp. 800–9.

Ahern, John (1989). "L'aquila tra gli indiani: le traduzioni americane di Dante." *Lettere Classensi* 18, pp. 211–34.

Ahern, John (1997). "Singing the Book: Orality in the Reception of Dante's *Comedy*." In A. Iannucci (ed.), *Dante: Contemporary Perspectives*. Toronto: University of Toronto Press, pp. 214–39.

Ahern, John (2003). "What Did the First Copies of the Comedy Look Like?" In T. Barolini and H. Wayne Storey (eds.), *Dante for the New Millennium*. New York: Fordham University Press, pp. 1–15.

Altrocchi, Rudolph (1931). "Michelino's Dante." *Speculum* 6, pp. 15–59.

Anderson, William (1982). *Dante the Maker*. New York: Crossroad.

Baranski, Zygmunt G. (1997). "Dante and Medieval Poetics." In A. Iannucci (ed.), *Dante: Contemporary Perspectives*. Toronto: University of Toronto Press, pp. 3–20.

Barbi, Michele (1954). *Life of Dante*, trans. and ed. Paul Ruggiers. Berkeley: University of California Press.

Barnes, John C. and Cormac Ó Cuilleanáin (eds.) (1995). *Dante and the Middle Ages*. Published for the Foundation for Italian Studies University College, Dublin. Dublin: Irish Academic Press.

Barolini, Teodolinda (1992). *The Undivine Comedy: Detheologizing Dante*. Princeton, NJ: Princeton University Press.

Barolini, Teodolinda (1993)."Why Did Dante Write the Comedy? or The Vision Thing." *Dante Studies* CXI, pp. 1–8.

Barolini, Teodolinda and H. Wayne Storey (eds.) (2003). *Dante for the New Millennium*. New York: Fordham University Press.

Bemrose, Stephen (2000). *A New Life of Dante*. Exeter, UK: University of Exeter Press.

Birk, Sandow and Marcus Sanders (2003–5). *The Divine Comedy*. San Francisco: Chronicle Books.

Boccaccio, Giovanni (1974). *The Earliest Lives of Dante. Translated from the Italian of Giovanni Boccaccio and Lionardo Bruni Aretino*, trans James Robinson Smith. New York: Haskell House.

Bosco, Umberto and Giorgio Petrocchi (eds.) (1970–8). *Enciclopedia dantesca*, 5 vols. and appendix. Rome: Enciclopedia Italiana.

Braida, Antonella (2004). *Dante and the Romantics*. Basingstoke, UK: Palgrave Macmillan.

Brieger, Peter, Millard Meiss, and Charles S. Singleton (eds.) (1969). *Illuminated Manuscripts of the "Divine Comedy,"* 2 vols. London: Routledge & Kegan Paul.

Caesar, Michael (1989). *Dante, The Critical Heritage (1314(?)–1870)*. The Critical Heritage Series. London and New York: Routledge.

Carson, Ciaran (2002). *The "Inferno" of Dante Alighieri, a New Translation by Ciaran Carson*. London and New York: Granta Books.

Comparetti, Domenico (1997). *Vergil in the Middle Ages*, trans. E. F. M. Benecke, 2nd edn. with new introduction by Jan Ziolkowski. Princeton, NJ: Princeton University Press.

Cunningham, Gilbert F. (1966). *The "Divine Comedy" in English: A Critical Bibliography*, 2 vols. Edinburgh and London: Oliver and Boyd.

Curtius, Ernst Robert (1963). *European Literature and the Latin Middle Ages*, trans. Willard R. Trask. New York: Harper & Row.

Davis, Charles Till (1984). *"Dante's Italy" and Other Essays*. Philadelphia: University of Pennsylvania.

De Gubernatis, Angelo (1900). *Fibre. Pagine di ricordi*. Rome: Forzani.

Douay-Rheims Version (1971). *The Holy Bible*. Rockford, IL: Tan Books.

Eliot, T. S. (1969). *The Complete Poems and Plays of T. S. Eliot*. London: Faber and Faber.

Ellis, Steven (1983). *Dante and English Poetry*. Cambridge, UK: Cambridge University Press.

Emerson, Ralph Waldo (1960). The *Journals of Ralph Waldo Emerson*, abridged and ed. Robert N. Linscott. New York: The Modern Library.

Ferrante, Joan M. (1984). *Political Vision of the "Divine Comedy."* Princeton, NJ: Princeton University Press.

Ferrante, Joan M. (1992). "Dante's Beatrice, Priest of an Androgynous God." Occasional Papers 2, Center for Medieval & Early Renaissance Studies. Binghamton, NY: Medieval & Renaissance Texts & Studies.

Foster, Kenelm and Patrick Boyde (1967). *Dante's Lyric Poetry*, 2 vols. Oxford: Clarendon Press.

Gardiner, Eileen (1989). *Visions of Heaven & Hell Before Dante*. New York: Italica Press.

Gillerman, Dorothy (1988). "Dante's Early Readers: The Evidence of Illustrated Manuscripts." In Giuseppe Di Scipio and Aldo Scaglione (eds.), *The Divine Comedy and the Encyclopedia of Arts and Sciences. Acta of the International Dante Symposium, 13–16 November 1983, Hunter College, New York*. Amsterdam and Philadelphia: John Benjamins, pp. 65–80.

Gilson, Simon (2005). *Dante and Renaissance Florence*. Cambridge, UK: Cambridge University Press.

Griffiths, Eric and Reynolds, Matthew (eds.) (2005). *Dante in English*. London: Penguin.

Hadfield, Alice Mary (1983). *Charles Williams: An Exploration of His Life and Work*. New York: Oxford University Press.

Havely, Nick (ed.) (1998), *Dante's Modern Afterlife: Reception and Response from Blake to Heaney*. New York: St. Martin's Press.

Havely, Nick (2003). " 'An Italian Writer Against the Pope?' Dante in Reformation England, c. 1560–1640." In E. G. Haywood (ed.), *Dante Metamorphoses*: *Episodes in a Literary Afterlife*. Dublin: Four Courts Press, pp. 127–49

Hawkins, Peter S. (1999). *Dante's Testaments: Essays in Scriptural Imagination*. Stanford, CA: Stanford University Press.

Hawkins, Peter S. and Rachel Jacoff (eds.) (2001). *The Poets' Dante: Twentieth-Century Responses*. New York: Farrar, Straus and Giroux.

Hawkins, Peter S. and Rachel Jacoff (2003). "Still Here: Dante after Modernism." In T. Barolini and H. Wayne Storey (eds.), *Dante for the New Millennium*. New York: Fordham University Press, pp. 451–64.

Haywood, Eric G. (ed.) (2003). *Dante Metamorphoses: Episodes in a Literary Afterlife*. Dublin: Four Courts Press.

Heaney, Seamus (1985). *Station Island*. New York: Farrar, Straus and Giroux.

Heaney, Seamus (2003)."Envies and Identifications: Dante and the Modern Poet." In P. S. Hawkins and R. Jacoff, *The Poets' Dante*. New York: Farrar, Straus and Giroux, pp. 239–58.

Hollander, Robert (2001). *Dante, A Life in Works*. New Haven, CT: Yale University Press.

Holmes, George (1980). *Dante*. Oxford: Oxford University Press.

Iannucci, Amilcare A. (1979–80). "Limbo: The Emptiness of Time." *Studi Danteschi* 52, pp. 69–128.

Iannucci, Amilcare A. (ed.) (1997). *Dante: Contemporary Perspectives*. Toronto: University of Toronto Press.

Iannucci, Amilcare A. (ed.) (2004a). *Dante, Cinema and Television*. Toronto: University of Toronto Press.

Iannucci, Amilcare A. (2004b). "Dante and Hollywood." In A. Iannucci (ed.), *Dante, Cinema and Television*. Toronto: University of Toronto Press, pp. 3–20.

Jacoff, Rachel (ed.) (1993). *The Cambridge Companion to Dante*. Cambridge, UK: Cambridge University Press.

Keen, Catherine (2003). *Dante and the City*. Stroud, UK: Tempus.

Lansing, Richard (ed.) (2000). *Dante Encyclopedia*. New York: Garland.

Lansing, Richard (ed.) (2003). *Dante: The Critical Complex*, 8 vols. London and New York: Routledge.

La Piana, Angelina (1948). *Dante's American Pilgrimage: A Historical Survey of Dante Studies in the United States, 1800–1944*. New Haven, CT, and London: Yale University Press.

Le Goff, Jacques (1986). *The Birth of Purgatory*, trans. Arthur Goldhammer. Chicago: University of Chicago Press.

Leo, Ulrich (1951). "The Unfinished 'Convivio' and Dante's Rereading of the 'Aeneid,' " *Medieval Studies* 13, pp. 41–64.

Lesnick, Daniel R. (1989). *Preaching in Medieval Florence: The Social World of Franciscan and Dominican Spirituality*. Athens, GA: University of Georgia Press.

Lewis, R. W. B. (1995). *The City of Florence: Historical Vistas and Personal Sightings*. New York: Farrar, Straus, and Giroux.

Lewis, R. W. B. (2001). *Dante*. New York: Lipper/Viking.

McDougal, Stuart Y. (ed.) (1985). *Dante Among the Moderns*. Chapel Hill, NC: University of North Carolina.

Meek, Christine (1995). "Dante's Life in His Times." In J. C. Barnes and C. Ó Cuilleanáin, *Dante and the Middle Ages*. Dublin: Irish Academic Press, pp. 11–31.

Milbank, Alison (1998). *Dante and the Victorians*. Manchester, UK: Manchester University Press.

Morgan, Alison (1990). *Dante and the Medieval Other World*. Cambridge, UK: Cambridge University Press.

Nussbaum, Martha C. (2001). *Upheavals of Thought: The Intelligence of Emotions*. Cambridge, UK: Cambridge University Press.

Panter, Gary (2005). *Jimbo in Purgatory*. San Francisco: Fantagraphics.

Pearl, Matthew (1999). " 'Colossal Cipher': Emerson as America's Lost Dantean." *Dante Studies* CXVII, pp. 171–94

Pertile, Lino (2003). "Does the Stilnovo Go to Heaven?" In T. Barolini and H. Wayne Storey (eds.), *Dante for the New Millennium*. New York: Fordham University Press, pp. 104–14.

Petrucci, Armando (1995). *Writers and Readers in Medieval Italy: Studies in the History of Written Culture*, ed. and trans. Charles M. Radding. New Haven, CT: Yale University Press.

Phillips, Tom (1992). *Works and Texts*. London: Thames and Hudson.

Pite, Ralph (1994). *The Circle of our Vision: Dante's Presence in English Romantic Poetry*. Oxford: Clarendon Press.

Psaki, F. Regina (2000). "The Sexual Body in Dante's Celestial Paradise." In Jan S. Emerson and Hugh Feiss, OSB (eds.), *Imagining Heaven in the Middle Ages: A Book of Essays*. New York: Garland, pp. 47–61.

Psaki, F. Regina (2003). "Love for Beatrice: Transcending Contradiction in the *Paradiso*." In T. Barolini and H. Wayne Storey (eds.), *Dante for the New Millennium*. New York: Fordham University Press, pp. 115–39

Reynolds, Barbara (1989). *The Passionate Intellect: Dorothy L. Sayers' Encounter with Dante*. Kent, OH, and London: Kent State University Press.

Ruskin, John (1898). *The Stones of Venice*, 3 vols. London: George Allen.

Salvatori, Corinna (2003). "Landmarks in the Fortunes of Dante in the Florentine Quattrocento." In E. G. Haywood (ed.), *Dante Metamorphoses*. Dublin: Four Courts Press, pp. 43–69.

Scott, John A. (2004). *Understanding Dante*. Notre Dame, IN: University of Notre Dame Press.

Shelley, Percy Bysshe (1977). *Shelley's Poetry and Prose. Authoritative Texts Criticism*, sel. and ed. David H. Reiman. New York: W. W. Norton.

Shideler, Mary McDermott (1966). *The Theology of Romantic Love: A Study in the Writings of Charles Williams*. Grand Rapids, MI: William B. Eerdmans.

Singleton, Charles S. (1958a). *An Essay on the "Vita Nuova."* Cambridge, MA: Harvard University Press.

Singleton, Charles S. (1958b). *Dante Studies 2: Journey to Beatrice*. Cambridge, MA: Harvard University Press.

Starn, Randolph (1982). *Contrary Commonwealth: The Theme of Exile in Medieval and Renaissance Italy*. Berkeley and Los Angeles: University of California Press.

Swanson, N. R. (1995). *Religion and Devotion in Europe, c. 1215–c. 1515*. Cambridge, UK: Cambridge University Press.

Taylor, Andrew (2004). "Television, Translation, and Vulgarization: Reflections on Phillips' and Greenaway's *A TV Dante*." In A. A. Iannucci (ed.), *Dante, Cinema and Television*. Toronto: University of Toronto Press, pp. 145–52.

Taylor, Charles H. and Patricia Finley (1997). *Images of the Journey in Dante's "Divine Comedy."* New Haven, CT, and London: Yale University Press.

Toynbee, Paget (1909). *Dante in English Literature*, 2 vols. London: Methuen.

Valency, Maurice (1958). *In Praise of Love: An Introduction to the Love-Poetry of the Renaissance*. New York: Macmillan.

Vauchez, André (1993). *The Laity in the Middle Ages: Religious Beliefs and Devotional Practices*, ed. D. E. Bornstein, trans. M. J. Schneider. Notre Dame, IN: University of Notre Dame Press.

Vickers, Nancy J. (1995). "Dante in the Video Decade." In Theodore J. Cachey, Jr. (ed.), *Dante Now: Current Trends in Dante Studies*. Notre Dame, IN: University of Notre Dame Press, pp. 263–76.

Waley, Daniel (1988). *The Italian City-Republics*, 3rd edn. London and New York: Longman.

Wallace, David (1993). "Dante in English." In R. Jacoff (ed.), *Cambridge Companion to Dante*. Cambridge, UK: Cambridge University Press, pp. 237–58.

Williams, Charles (1941). *Religion and Love in Dante: The Theology of Romantic Love*. London: Dacre Press.

Williams, Charles (1961). *The Figure of Beatrice: A Study in Dante*. New York: Noonday/Farrar, Straus & Cudahy.

Index

Inferno (cont'd)
  as meditation on
      Incarnation 110–11
  outline 33–5
  sources of imagery 39–42
  and Virgil as guide 35–9
intellect 63, 85–6
  see also knowledge
irony 40–1, 156
Ireland, and Dante 137; *see also*
      Northern Ireland
Italy, and reception of Dante
      xvi–xvii, 24–5, 142,
      150–1, 152

Jerusalem
  on Dante's world map *30*, 31
  heavenly 32
Joachim of Fiore 102–3
joy, in the Trinity 123
Joyce, James 137, 145, 147, 148,
      156
justice, divine 36–9, 45–7, 53, 109
Justinian, Emperor 63, 65, 126

Kallman, Chester 95–7
Keats, John 140
Keillor, Garrison 65
knowledge
  desire for 106–7
  of God 33, 70, 77, 98, 107
  see also intellect

laity
  and education 102
  and religious life 104–5
language

and the ineffable 62, 68–9,
      112, 121
  sensual 84–8
Latin, literary language 14
Latini, Brunetto 11, 38, 146
laudesi (devotional groups) 104
lectura Dantis tradition 26–7,
      152
Lesnick, Daniel R. 172 n.3
Lethe (river) 32, 59, 126
Lewis, C. S. 145
light
  and Paradise 64, 116, 121–2, 126
  and Purgatory 47–8, 124
Limbo 170 n.7, *see also*
      Purgatory, and virtuous
      pagans
literature, impact of Dante on
      136–8, 145–8
Longfellow, Henry Wadsworth
      143
love
  courtly 7, 92, 97, 126
  and divine glory 7–8, 59
  effects in Purgatory 53–4, 67
  and Eros 71, 82–3
  homosexual 94–7
  married 90
  and theology 93–7, 106
Lowell, James Russell 143
Lowell, Robert 145
Lucy, St 36
Luzi, Mario 153

Macaulay, Thomas
      Babbington 141
Malebolge 42, 166

Lightning Source UK Ltd.
Milton Keynes UK
UKOW06f2138080615

253106UK00009B/52/P